Notes From the Margins

Notes From the Margins

Reflections on Regimes of Knowledge and Power

Amardo J. Rodriguez

Copyright © 2015 by Amardo J. Rodriguez

All rights reserved. No part of this publication may be reproduced, distributed, or transmitted in any form or by any means, including photocopying, recording, or other electronic or mechanical methods, without the prior written permission of the publisher, except in the case of brief quotations embodied in critical reviews and certain other noncommercial uses permitted by copyright law. For permission requests, write to the publisher, addressed "Attention: Permissions Coordinator," at the address below.

ISBN: 0692488316
ISBN: 9780692488317

Public Square Press
309 Fayette Drive
Fayetteville, NY 13066
USA

For
Joshua and Jordan

Contents

	Prologue	ix
Chapter 1	On The End of Identity	1
Chapter 2	The Limits of Pedagogy	17
Chapter 3	On Metaphors and Knowledge	21
Chapter 4	On The Coming Singularity	25
Chapter 5	On Modern Philosophy	41
Chapter 6	On The Nature of Theory	46
Chapter 7	On War and Peace	49
Chapter 8	On The Limits of Education	52
Chapter 9	On The Nature of Ideology	57
Chapter 10	On Rights and Obligations	79
Chapter 11	On Whiteness Studies	83
Chapter 12	On Defining Theory	89
Chapter 13	On Diversity and Identity	94
Chapter 14	On Being and Knowing	101
Chapter 15	On Language and Mind	113
Chapter 16	On The Limits of Theory	125
Chapter 17	On The End of Truth	131
Chapter 18	On The Politics of Diversity	138
Chapter 19	On The End of Violence	141
Chapter 20	On Valuing Objectivity	145
Chapter 21	On The Rise of Civilizations	150
Chapter 22	On The Nature of Institutions	153

Chapter 23 On Human Rights · 162
Chapter 24 On Democracy and Government · 169
Chapter 25 On The Limits of Science · 175
            References · 179
            About the Author · 181

Prologue

THERE IS NOTHING NATURAL ABOUT writing. In order to write we must devise either reasons or illusions to do so. We have to convince ourselves that writing matters. It is worthy of the anguish. But what happens when finding a compelling enough reason to write becomes impossible? On the other hand, what happens when we are unable to release ourselves of the impulse to write? How do we navigate this conflict? I have always come to writing assuming that knowledge matters. To write is to produce knowledge, which in turn will presumably make the world better. Writing is therefore an important activity. It is deserving of the anguish, and all else that comes with it.

This book has much of that kind of anguish. But it is also laden with a different kind of anguish. Does the world really need more knowledge? Would more knowledge save us from ourselves? In fact, do ideas really matter? Do ideas make for moral evolution? In other words, does the world really need more writing, and thereby another article, another book? What can we now promise to write about that is new or more important than something already written? So throughout the writing of this book I have anguished, and anguished again. As much as I can find no compelling reason to write, I still must write. Writing is where I make sense of everything. It is where I converse with the world. I am never forsaken in writing. Writing always leaves me in a better place. The anguish is never in vain.

I also now have a better understanding of the process. Vulnerability is vital. Only by being vulnerable will the world converse with us. I have come to understand this the hard way, though my learning continues. The point

I am trying to make is that I will make no case that this book is important. It speaks merely to my own desperate need to converse honestly and courageously with the world. Most times I had no clue as to how the process will play out. Often I wrote blindly and desperately. But again, I was never forsaken. This book is about my attempt to make sense of a world that makes no sense. For how does the invention and proliferation of weapons of mass destruction make sense? How does our destruction of our own habitat make sense? How does the mass incarceration of millions for nonviolent offenses make sense? How does the institutionalization of learning make sense? How does any kind of fundamentalism make sense in a world laden with ambiguity and mystery? Barely anything in this world makes sense. How did this come to be? How did we come to create a world that makes no sense?

I continue to write because I am in search of a world that makes sense. I need to believe that such a world (or worlds) is possible, meaning that we are potentially capable of creating a better world. Sometimes what we are capable of believing and imagining is much more valuable than what we are capable of achieving and materializing. But what would a world that made sense look like? What does the making of such a world demand of us? Finally, and most importantly, what does the possibility of such a world reveal about our origins and purpose? These are the questions that brought this book into being and make for my own reasons for writing.

CHAPTER 1
ON THE END OF IDENTITY

IDENTITY IS A SACRED CONCEPT in any discussion of diversity. We are to assume that identity matters. It is presumably foundational to any progressive politics. No doubt, many persons have a vested interest in having us continue to assume that identity matters. We presumably need to resist efforts to downplay our differences, and claims that our differences impede us coming together and working on problems that affect all of us. We must contend that identity matters because differences matter.

But for whom, and for what, and why? If identity matters, how, with the political rise of so many persons from minority backgrounds, to explain the new Jim Crow that is upon us with so many women and minority persons in prison for nonviolent offenses? How also to explain the complicity of the Black community, the Latino community, the Native American community, and women in the making of this new Jim Crow? On the other hand, can identity save us from the ecological peril that is now upon us? Can identity save us from the impending collapse of global capitalism? Can identity stop the proliferation of weapons of mass destruction? Can identity save us from the coming water crisis? In sum, what is the promise of identity in a world that is increasingly fraught with peril? This peril has no regards to identity. So, again, why this fixation with identity?

The Problem with Boxes

We are to believe that identity is vital to diversity. To lose our identity is supposedly to lose what makes us different. Identity supposedly captures our differences. It reflects what lives and experiences are absent, and thereby need to be included. But what is emancipatory about inclusion? Does the addition and inclusion of differences promise the emancipation of the oppressed, the marginalized, and the downtrodden? Inclusion means accommodation, absorption, and assimilation. But how can diversity be included and accommodated and still be diversity?

Inclusion degrades diversity, diminishes diversity, depoliticizes diversity, emasculates diversity, neutralizes diversity. It reduces diversity to a box, limiting what diversity can potentially become. Every box constitutes a fundamental distortion of diversity. Boxes are social constructs—born out of the need to impose order on the world. That is, boxes are born purely out of social forces. Understanding the origins of these forces is vital to understanding how boxes are supposed to work and for what purposes. Moreover, boxes diminish our complexity, diversity, mystery, and ultimately our humanity by reducing us to units that can be sorted like oranges and apples. Our complexity and diversity come from the fact that human beings are relational, sexual, spiritual, physical, material, historical, sensual, emotional, existential, ecological, primal, geographical, and cultural beings. Downplaying or missing this complexity and diversity presents serious problems. Our identity exceeds any one dimension. We could be of the same sexual orientation, but be of fundamentally different social, political, spiritual, material, historical, cultural, and epistemological persuasions. Besides the fact that these different dimensions shape and influence each other, these different dimensions are also bound up with each other.

Downplaying or missing our complexity and diversity also tends to make believe that only one dimension is most important to us (such as our sexual orientation). But the person of a certain box (in this case sexual orientation) is also a son/daughter, brother/sister, aunt/uncle, niece/nephew, friend/colleague, Democrat/Republican, communist/capitalist/anarchist, Christian/Buddhist/Methodist/Hindu/atheist, working class/middle class/upper class, and so forth. Further, reducing our complexity and diversity reduces the totality of a person's humanity by reducing the person to only one dimension (in this case, sexual orientation) and usually the dimension that matters to others. This process allows for the beginnings of processes that dehumanize and denigrate. Also, boxes promote stereotyping. We are all different by the fact that our many dimensions (social, cultural, historical, material, geographical) will always be different. We will react to the world differently, deal with the world differently, interpret the world differently, and view the world differently. Checking the same box means absolutely nothing. In addition, boxes perpetuate our fear and suspicion of confusion. We all but demand that persons fit neatly into a box or simply choose a box. Also, boxes promote conformity and stereotyping by attaching certain expectations to different boxes. Moreover, boxes promote mystification and alienation by keeping us bound to the expectations that come with different boxes. That is, boxes block us from exploring what resides beyond the confines and borders of boxes, meaning that boxes discourage us from exploring various instincts, impulses, and desires. Finally, boxes impede communication by impeding our own capacity to deal with a world that is laden with confusion. The goal of boxes is to make the world neat and tidy. But this is our ambition. Nothing about the world is neat, tidy, or even easy. Confusion is the order of things, and communication is the only way through confusion. Yet no amount of communication can ever end confusion. Again, confusion is the order of things. Communication merely represents the most constructive way of navigating and grappling with the world's confusion. So in trying to end confusion, boxes limit and diminish communication.

Inclusion stops diversity from disrupting the status quo. It undermines any possibility of a full emancipation for those who have been historically oppressed, brutalized, and marginalized. This is also how identity protects the status quo from the threat of revolution. Nurturing this possibility of revolution requires diversity to defy the seduction of inclusion and accommodation. It must remain on the margins, in the badlands. It must remain excluded, always contesting and challenging all that the status quo values to be good, just, and decent. Anything that can be included and accommodated is something other than diversity. Diversity must always contain the possibility of a new vision of the world. It must always pose a threat to the order of things. Identity has nothing to do with diversity. Diversity is about the cultivation of possibility. It is about nurturing practices and ways of being that promise to expand our view of the world. This is how and why diversity is life affirming. The absence of diversity means the absence of beauty, vitality, and creativity. Diversity is a life catalyst. It is inherently emancipatory.

Identity impedes diversity. By obstructing the evolution of diversity, identity gives us plurality rather than diversity. Plurality is about addition, inclusion, and accommodation of our supposed differences. It is about imposing speech codes and various norms of civility and collegiality for supposedly the sake of accommodating our differences. Plurality reduces diversity to charity, such as affirmative action. This is why the politics of inclusion wants nothing to do with reparations. Reparations are about justice rather than charity. Plurality reduces diversity to agreement, such as our agreeing to be civil to each other, nice to each other, charitable to each other. There must be no offensive speech or conduct. But what are the cultural and ideological origins of this civility and normativity that diversity must obediently submit to? Whose interests are best served by this civility and normativity? That is, who benefits from the suppression of conflict and the rage that has been smoldering for over 350 years? Why should such a rage be suppressed through a false and disingenuous civility? No doubt, this civility and collegiality constitutes a most effective disciplinary device. Yet for those who are always teaching and writing about disciplinary devices, there remains a curious omission of this device. Then again, this is the device that such persons are always employing to limit diversity. Again and again diversity must deal with such disciplining for supposedly the sake of maintaining civility. Nobody, of course, will ever profess to being against diversity. We merely demand that diversity be civil and collegial. But in order for diversity to be diversity, diversity must challenge all of our norms, including our norms of civility and collegiality. For what is ultimately lost in the suppression of our rage is the truth. Diversity is most insidiously compromised by our failure or unwillingness to deal with the truth. Dealing with the truth demands hearing what we are unwilling to hear, and knowing what we are unwilling to know.

Diversity is about possessing the courage to embody the truth. This is why diversity will always face harassment and persecution. Nothing poses as much a threat to the status quo as the truth. Our norms of civility and collegiality aim to suppress the truth. But any attempt to limit the truth only distorts and diminishes the truth. Truth must be unbound, which means that diversity must also be unbound. This much is evident in the story of Jesus Christ. This is ultimately a compelling story of diversity. It captures both the tribulations and perils of diversity. Persecution is inevitable as diversity is morally and epistemologically obligated to challenge the dominant regimes of truth that sustain various structures of power and privilege. Thus, in the case of Jesus Christ, the crime was sedition, threatening the integrity of the status quo. So although Jesus Christ never posed a military threat to the status quo, those in power intuitively knew that the truth can bring down empires. This is why the penalty had to be death. Such threats must be dealt with harshly in order to protect the status quo. On the other hand, threatening the integrity of the status quo is what diversity is morally and epistemologically obligated to do. This is the measure of diversity. It must always contain the possibility of revolution. That is, diversity must always possess the possibility of a new way of viewing the world, understanding the world, experiencing the world, and engaging the world. This, again, is why diversity cannot be included, and should never seek to be included.

The politics of inclusion opposes diversity, conspires against diversity, seeks to diminish diversity. It celebrates a diversity that poses no threat to the status quo. Diversity is reduced to colors, flavors, and festivals, with a focus on recognizing, embracing, bridging, and celebrating our rainbow of differences. The common assumption being that the inclusion of diversity is a good thing. What emerges from the politics of inclusion is a belief that only certain kinds of diversity are tolerable, those that can be recognized, embraced, and bridged and thereby can be included in our rainbow of diversity and multiculturalism. Other kinds of diversity become fair game for contempt and persecution. But why should diversity be bridged and included? Why is this necessary in order for diversity to be good and saved from contempt and persecution? Simply put, why should diversity be tolerable, and thereby willing to submit to prevailing norms? Was Jesus Christ seeking to be tolerable? If so, why the sword? *"Do not think that I came to bring peace on earth. I did not come to bring peace but a sword"* (Matthew 10:34). But this is how the politics of inclusion diminishes, compromises, and depoliticizes diversity. We are to simply assume that inclusion is good, and anything that impedes inclusion is supposedly bad. As such, initiatives that support inclusion are good, and those that do differently are supposedly bad. However, history offers no compelling case for inclusion, especially for peoples who have been historically brutalized and disenfranchised.

Inclusion means superiority. We are willing to be recognized and embraced by those different to us, actually by those who long judged us to be less than human. We are also willing to be judged and evaluated by the standards and values of others, implicitly acknowledging that those values and standards are superior to our own. Yet even after doing all of this inclusion remains beyond our reach. We never gain the respect that our colleagues attain. Our achievements and accomplishments are always suspect. We are never fully on the inside. There are always hints that we are seeking to be included into a system that *really* belongs to others. The values and standards that we prize and cherish belong to others. We apparently have none of our own. Or, what we have is inferior. This is why, after all, we are seeking to be included. Eventually this reality is upon us. We will never be fully included. The system will never work for us. The master's tools will always be the master's tools. We will always be outsiders.

Then there is the existential and spiritual cost we continue to pay to be included, such as agreeing to abide by all manner of illusions. How could a journal's impact factor be a measure of a person's truth? In fact, how could quantity be a factor in determining a person's contribution to the betterment of humankind? How many books did Jesus Christ or Moses produce? How could the value of a person's teaching be reduced to a number? How did perceptual reasoning index, working memory index, and processing speed index become variables in determining the capacity of a human being to learn, imagine, and innovate? Indeed, how did any standardized test become a measure of a person's potentiality? Such are only a few of the illusions that inclusion requires of us. But there are always illusions. The reason being that the politics of inclusion begins on an illusion—the illusion being that the world is inherently of an intractable conflict between benevolent forces (e.g., life, order, health, meaning, knowledge, communication) and malevolent forces (e.g., death, chaos, disease, ambiguity, ignorance, confusion). Consequently, as much as this politics professes to value diversity, embrace diversity, celebrate diversity, the goal of this politics is unity. It will always possess a suspicion of diversity. This is why this politics insists on tropes like civility and collegiality so as to stop diversity from causing mischief and mayhem.

Inclusion means unity, commonality, and similarity. It is about coming together, finding common ground, recognizing our shared goals, working together, protecting our common interests, appreciating our common humanity. The civility and collegiality that inclusion promotes presupposes the sharing of a common sensibility, as well as a common rationality. But what of Jesus Christ's tumbling of the money-changing stalls in the temple? By whose standards were such actions civil? Inclusion will never pose a threat to the status quo. In valuing unity, commonality, and similarity, inclusion privileges order, meaning, and stability. In fact, inclusion is a creature of this ideology that assumes that the world is of an intractable conflict between supposedly benevolent and malevolent forces. Inclusion is merely a mechanism this ideology uses to protect the status quo from diversity. However, because the status quo cannot end diversity, inclusion is about co-opting diversity. This is how the politics of inclusion succeeds in professing to value diversity, even celebrate diversity, but is really about neutralizing diversity.

DIVERSITY AND DEFINITIONS

As with all politics, definitions matter. Who defines what will shape how the politics unfold. Diversity is supposedly about race, gender, sexuality, nationality, and disability. This is also how we frame identity. But what is the value of defining identity this way? Why these groupings, and why even the need for groupings? What is heuristic about these groupings, and the use of groupings as a whole? Evidently, groupings mean unity, commonality, and similarity. Groupings mean that these are my people. These are the people who presumably share my ethics and politics. But of course such unity, commonality, and similarity are usually illusory. There is also the diversity of our histories, rationalities, sensibilities, modalities, and spiritualities. There is diversity in our theories, methodologies, and pedagogies. The point being that our diversity exceeds our common groupings. Such groupings limit and distort our diversity, and consequently also distort our conception of self. In the end, our common notions of diversity and identity disfigure our humanity by cultivating narcissism and obsession with our own kind.

Narcissism is the origin of all racism, tribalism, nationalism, fundamentalism, and ethnocentrism. Without narcissism, the world will be spared the ravages of such evils. As such, what business does the oppressed have in also conceiving of identity in terms of narcissism? The oppressed, the marginalized, the downtrodden, and the forsaken need a new conception of personhood. We need a vision of personhood that has no origin in either similarity or commonality. This means a conception of personhood that orients us towards those who seem most different to us, even those who trespass against us. Such a conception is found in the teachings of Jesus Christ. Our foremost concern is about the well-being of others. We are what we help others to become. This is a relational view of being. Such a view begins on the premise that our humanity is bound up with the humanity of others. Consequently, the condition of my humanity is bound up with the condition of your humanity. We are therefore to love our neighbor as much as we love ourselves.

But the politics of inclusion would have us assume that the problems that plague us are racism, sexism, ableism, and heterosexism. This is supposedly why the full inclusion of diversity is yet to be achieved. We are to commit ourselves to rooting out these evils. We generally view these evils in terms of hostility towards those of different groups. We focus on stamping out these evils, such as removing the hostility towards the other groups. The politics of inclusion wants us to fight these evils. We are to assume that these evils reside in various biases and prejudices. Our goal is to find the origins of these biases and prejudices. We are to assume that these evils are responsible for our failure to achieve a fully inclusive society. We charge persons for being complicit in tolerating and encouraging racism, sexism, and heterosexism. We point to various practices as being racist. But all of this commotion is nothing but a diversion.

Narcissism is the enemy of diversity. Narcissism means fixation with self, obsession with self. It also means moral and emotional retardation, such as lacking the capacity to view and experience the world from the position of others. Accordingly, narcissism also means selfishness and a lack of empathy and compassion. It constitutes the origins of our own moral failures by impeding our ability to view the world from positions that are fundamentally different to our own. This is why racism constitutes a diversion, merely a way of excusing our own narcissism. As long as narcissism remains in place, racism, sexism, and heterosexism will have safe refuge. These evils make for an easy politics. We merely have to point, condemn, and march to end racism. But saving the world from narcissism is hard. The only way to do so is by disrupting and changing everything, beginning with our relation to others. As such, the politics of inclusion has an interest in making us believe that our problems are racism, sexism, and heterosexism. Fixing and solving these problems poses no threat to anything. Even better, these problems are increasingly seen in medical terms. Counseling is supposedly the most effective way to deal with our racial issues. Now, our goal is to identify racism without racists, sexism without sexists, heterosexism without heterosexists—exposing the biases and prejudices that supposedly reside deep in our subconscious. But again, nothing about this politics poses a threat to anything.

We can afford to give up a few racists, sexists, and heterosexists for supposedly the sake of achieving inclusion. We can even toss in a few affirmative action positions and resources for the sake of inclusion. The goal of the politics of inclusion is to limit diversity. This means stopping diversity from causing any disruption that could threaten the status quo. Diversity must never get to the level of worldview, the worldview that ideologically and epistemologically nurtures the status quo. However, it is only at the level of worldviews that revolutions begin and happen. Thus by refusing to deal with the worldview that nurtures the status quo, the politics of inclusion has already acknowledged that revolution is off limits. Only inclusion is an option, meaning that only a shallow and narrow view of diversity will be included and accommodated. What then does the complicity of minority peoples in the legitimizing of this politics of inclusion mean for the promise of diversity? In sum, what becomes of the possibility of emancipation and liberation when the slave insists on using the tools of the master?

What now passes for diversity functions as a kind of rearguard, protecting the status quo from diversity. The rise of diversity means the end of all the institutions that are supposedly about the promotion of diversity and supposedly reflect our commitment to diversity. It also involves the rise of a new consciousness, which means a new way of looking at self and personhood. But most of all, the rise of diversity involves the rise of a new worldview, including all the practices that come with a new worldview. The politics of inclusion constitutes the most insidious threat to diversity. It allows the status quo to use slave against slave.

Resources are supposedly the demands of diversity. We want all the resources necessary to achieve our full inclusion. Every supposed diversity incident comes with a list of new demands, including the need for new regulations, new laws, new committees, new positions. We are to assume that with enough resources and complementary institutional support, inclusion will be ours. We merely have to keep agitating, organizing, and marching. But the politics of inclusion will always disappoint as no amount of resources will achieve our inclusion.

Diversity requires a politics of liberation. For what is diversity? It is the affirmation of possibility, the nurturing of new ways of understanding and experiencing the world that enlarges our vision of the world. A politics of liberation is about cultivating and promoting practices that nurture possibility. Possibility is life. Diversity is an expression of possibility. It is about enlarging what is possible rather than merely acknowledging what is different. What possibilities are we suppressing or precluding when we value or believe or assume one thing or another? Such is the problem with the politics of inclusion. Everything it values, believes, and assumes impedes possibility. We are to assume that diversity begins with race, ethnicity, gender, sexuality, and disability. But does this diversity promise us new ways of viewing the world? Historically, no such case can be made. What, therefore, is the value of these groupings in terms of promoting diversity? Indeed, such groups have been historically excluded. But was exclusion the real evil?

DIVERSITY AND EXCLUSION

Our exclusion was merely an expression of a much larger abomination that had nothing to do with our supposed differences. This abomination was a crime against all of humanity. What now passes for exclusion is really about the subjugation of possibility, and consequently, the subjugation of life. All of the great evils, whether slavery, Jim Crow, apartheid, the Holocaust, had nothing to do with our differences. But to look at these abominations in terms of differences distorts our full understanding of these evils, as well as our recognizing of what is responsible for these evils. There is no implication of worldviews, such as the worldview that continues to rule our world, and ruled our world then. Yes, the worldview that ruled the world then is also the worldview that rules the world now. So again, how could the worldview that makes for so much oppression be also the worldview of emancipation and liberation? To use Audre Lorde's words, how could the tools that build the house of the master also build the house of the slave?

Slavery, Jim Crow, and other such evils had nothing to do with exclusion. If African Americans were simply excluded over the last few hundred years, then inclusion suffices as a remedy. What was systematically excluded should now be favorably included. But African Americans were by no means merely excluded. African Americans were enslaved, tortured, brutalized, and murdered. The politics of inclusion masks this reality by assuming that the problem was exclusion. This is supposedly the problem that now needs fixing. We are never challenged by the politics of inclusion to fully account for the ideological and epistemological origins of slavery and Jim Crow, including all the legal, social, political, institutional, and epistemological practices that perpetuated these evils for over 350 years. We are to focus on achieving inclusion. We are to treat 350 years of slavery and Jim Crow as merely product of biases and prejudices, and nothing to do with ideology and epistemology. In other words, the origins of such evils supposedly have no ideological and epistemological bearing on the present. But such evils were by no means merely a product of various biases and prejudices. If only for the sake of our ancestors, a much better account of the origins of these evils is necessary. How did such brutality become morally and epistemologically permissible for over 350 years? What about our worldview that made for the perpetuation of all this misery and brutality?

Slavery and Jim Crow reveal a worldview that has no regard for life. This is a worldview of death. It conspires to limit possibility. This is why, in addition to diversity, this worldview is also hostile to liberty. It can only profess on paper to favor liberty. For again, at the foundation of this worldview is a belief that the world is of a violent conflict between supposedly benevolent and malevolent forces. Our survival and prosperity are presumably dependent on us subduing and limiting the latter. Consequently, malevolent forces bring us fear, dread, and anxiety. Anything that induces any of these forces becomes subject to a campaign of subjugation. Diversity will always be subject to such a campaign. As much as the politics of inclusion aims to lessen our fear of diversity, homogeneity will always be perceived as benevolent. This is why diversity must always be controlled and regulated and disciplined. It can never be unbound. Civility is necessary to bookend diversity. What emerges is a worldview that makes us increasingly afraid of anything that seems malevolent. Anything that causes us anxiety must be suppressed, controlled, and disciplined rather than recognized, engaged, and explored. In this way, this worldview increasingly cripples us by filling us with all manner of neuroses and psychoses. It diminishes our capacity to live honestly, transparently, and courageously, making for what psychologists now refer to as the reactive mind. Simply put, this worldview makes us cowards. We are constantly afraid, always tortured by anxiety. The world becomes a place of torment. The reactive mind is a violent mind. Unable to engage with the world openly and honestly, anything that induces any kind of fear or anxiety becomes a threat that must be put down violently. Our focus is on acquiring the means that will allow us to destroy any threat. Such is the desperation that is of the reactive mind. This is also how the reactive mind becomes immune to violence and the everyday ways we brutalize and dehumanize each other. It is also how the reactive mind legitimizes violence. Violence presumably saves us from everything that seems to threaten us.

The reactive mind is a weak mind. It needs order and structure to function. It values hierarchy. Hierarchy aspires to use redundant systems, practices, and structures, to limit diversity, ambiguity, and spontaneity. Its goal is conformity, stability, and predictability so as to save us from the malevolent forces that supposedly roam the world causing mischief and mayhem. However, as hierarchy emerges, the reactive mind becomes increasingly tortured and paralyzed. Every new level of control stops us from grappling and struggling with the ambiguity, complexity, and mystery that are necessary to make us strong and resilient. Hierarchy makes the reactive mind increasingly weak and fragile, and accordingly, increasingly afraid of anything that induces fear and anxiety. Through hierarchy the reactive mind becomes trapped. It cannot function without hierarchy, and is crippled by hierarchy. The reactive mind is devoid of any capacity to create, innovate, and imagine. It can only navigate the world through hierarchy. It values conformity above everything else, and is ready to do anything to achieve conformity, stability, and predictability. It has no patience or tolerance for dissent and discord. Anything that is different induces fear and anxiety. Such is the desperation for conformity that torments the reactive mind. But such is only the beginning of the ravages of hierarchy.

All of the systems, structures, and practices that come with hierarchy alienate and separate us from each other. We lose the ability to recognize our humanity in each other. Hierarchy divides us. To be afraid of anything that induces fear and anxiety is also to be afraid of anyone who induces fear and anxiety. But because of the separation that hierarchy creates we never have to reckon with all the misery that comes from the violence we use to achieve our conformity. Hierarchy removes us from the violence, including all the damage and carnage our violence is causing. However, because the separation that hierarchy fosters is illusory, what is lost is how all of this violence falls back on us, including all the damage and carnage. This is the most monstrous travesty that hierarchy inflicts on us. It turns us violently upon ourselves. No amount of inclusion can save us from this kind of self-destruction. In reality, slavery, Jim Crow, and other such evils had nothing to do with our differences and our supposed failure to recognize, embrace, and bridge our differences. The politics of inclusion perpetuates the illusion of our separation by assuming that our differences make us different. Thus the inclusion of race, ethnicity, gender, sexuality, and disability matters. Supposedly, such differences reflect our separation. This is why the politics of inclusion promotes the bridging of our differences, metaphorically treating us as being different land masses. Diversity presumably resides in our differences. To lose our differences is presumably to lose our diversity.

But there is no diversity in our differences. If diversity resides in our differences, then diversity resides in our separation and self-destruction. This is why the politics of inclusion leads to ideological incest. We increasingly demand the hiring and recruiting of our own kind and the building of our own programs and departments. We are to assume that by attending to our own interests we make the world better. After all, who else is going to attend to our issues? But how does narcissism get us to selflessness? The story of Jesus Christ reminds us that our redemption begins with our capacity to love those who are different to us, even those who wish to destroy us. For those who are different to us are never outside or separate from us.

Diversity and Redemption

To love is to heal from the damage that separation produces. Love promotes diversity. It promotes diversity by cultivating union and communion. In other words, love enlarges our humanity by locating the humanity of others in ours. There can be no concern for self without concern for others. Love nurtures diversity by saving diversity from violence. No doubt, love is hard. But this is how love strengthens us. If only the strong can forgive, then only the strongest can love. Love requires faith, enormous faith. We have to be ready to believe in things that most will never have the courage to imagine. Such faith requires enormous courage. But such is the courage that love requires. Such is also the courage that diversity requires. Diversity is an expression of love. Love brings diversity into the world. Love expands the realm of the possible. In love all things are possible. This is why the story of Jesus Christ constitutes such a compelling story of diversity. It is a story about love. It was love that made for the diversity of Jesus Christ. It was Jesus Christ's love that posed the greatest threat to the status quo.

Love distinguishes diversity from plurality. A theory of diversity must ultimately be a theory of love, and any politics of diversity must ultimately be a politics of love. Violence has no place in any politics of diversity. Yet violence characterizes the politics of inclusion. We demand that every perceived transgression be dealt with harshly and punitively so as to show our commitment to promoting diversity. Now those who have been historically brutalized call for the brutalizing of others. We too use violence to achieve our own kind of conformity in the name of promoting diversity. We must all agree on what is offensive and objectionable or else face contempt and retribution. We must all share the same outrage over certain incidents or else face contempt and retribution. As always, the politics of inclusion really wants nothing to do with diversity. It wants uniformity, conformity, and homogeneity. It wants us to remain beholden to the tools of the master. Rather than promoting diversity, the politics of inclusion is merely another way of bringing violence into the world. It is oblivious to the fact that violence only begets violence. But such is how morally, theoretically, and spiritually bankrupt is the politics of inclusion. By focusing on our differences, the politics of inclusion has the ideological permission of the status quo to keep the focus on differences. After all, our differences pose no threat to anything. We also like the notion of being entitled to be included, of demanding our fair share of the spoils. But what is our obligation to those who suffered over 350 years of slavery and Jim Crow? How does our inclusion stop the continuing shaming and brutalizing of the marginalized, the downtrodden, and the forsaken? Indeed, how did inclusion become a viable solution to the world's problems? Is inclusion the solution to the proliferation of weapons of mass destruction, or our destruction of the planet, or the widening gap between rich and poor? Thus why this obsession with inclusion? In reality, the politics of inclusion, besides protecting the ideological and epistemological integrity of the status quo, makes for an effective distraction. It constitutes a shallow understanding of everything. It also releases us from doing what is really hard. Our redemption ultimately depends on our ability to love. Only through love can the world be spared the ravages of violence. That the politics of inclusion would have us believe that through violence we can achieve diversity only demonstrates how absurd everything has now become. If diversity is really supposed to be something beautiful, something of the slave rather than the master, then diversity must come from something beautiful. That something can only be love. Only through love can we emancipate our beauty, potentiality, and diversity. Only through love can we enlarge and reimagine what is possible. Only through love can we save ourselves from ourselves.

So what then is love? Love is an act of imagination. To love is to believe in things that others simply lack the courage to believe. In other words, love requires the most courage a human being can muster. It reflects fortitude and resolve. To love is about the courage to love, the courage to believe, the courage to imagine. There is nothing that stretches us, pushes us, and challenges us as love. In doing all of these things, love enlarges what we are capable of understanding and experiencing. So regardless of the fact that different cultures have different ways of symbolizing love, what really matters is whether we are pushing and challenging what we are ready and willing to believe. Before love is moral, love is epistemological. It is a way of engaging the world. Through love the divide between the world and us collapses, just as much as the divide between others and us collapse. Through love the ideologies and epistemologies that cultivate these divides also collapse and implode. This is what makes love such a threat to the status quo. It changes our understanding, experiencing, and perceiving of everything.

CHAPTER 2

THE LIMITS OF PEDAGOGY

BEING DEGREED IS FUNDAMENTALLY DIFFERENT to being educated. Schooling is an institution, and institutions impede learning by demanding submission, subordination, and repetition. The mission of an institution is to maintain command and control through the deployment of various practices, structures, and arrangements. However, learning involves challenging our fears, beliefs, values, truths, and norms. It also involves challenging how we perceive and experience the world, and finding and achieving the resources necessary to reimagine all that is possible. In this way, learning involves challenging mind, body, and soul. It is about altering our ways of being in the world. We must be willing to experience the world anew, ourselves anew, each other anew. Learning can neither be forced nor coerced. Yet schooling would have us believe otherwise.

What now passes for learning is nothing but violence. Schooling encourages the notion that only through violence are we capable of being competent. It insidiously relegitimizes the belief that hierarchy is inevitable and necessary. Schooling involves no risk, no confusion and tribulation. It requires no disrupting of anything. Indeed, schooling poses no threat to anything. It makes us amenable to all the violence that every institution cultivates and needs. Besides desensitizing us to all the violence that is necessary to achieve our submission and subordination, schooling legitimizes all of this violence by making us believe that such violence, in promoting learning, is always serving a greater good.

But what to make of our own complicity in promoting all of this violence when we who teach in institutions of higher learning are supposed to be the most educated and learned? Evidently, we are anything but educated and learned. We are merely the most schooled, the most credentialed, the most institutionalized. We are the most dangerous element in the equation. That we are perceived as the most learned by the fact that we are the most schooled and credentialed also creates the impression that we are the most enlightened. Our supposed vast knowledge gives us a certain kind of authority to dictate to the masses how the world should be perceived and experienced. We exercise this authority by creating disciplines, shaping curriculums, and dictating the expectations for learning. We also exercise this authority through the creation of institutional apparatuses where we define and dictate what kinds of knowledge are appropriate and credible. Moreover, we exercise this authority by deciding who gets tenured and promoted, and thus who gets access to resources. Our authority functions institutionally, to protect the integrity of the institution that is schooling. It validates schooling as an institution that is vital to preserving the order of things. But again, such validation comes with much pretense, such as the pretense that schooling promotes learning, the pretense that school correlates with learning, the pretense that our supposed progress is a result of our increasing capacity to acquire and disseminate our knowledge, the pretense that scholars are really producing and disseminating knowledge, and the pretense that quantity of knowledge is vital to progress.

Writing matters to us because we believe that through writing we disseminate knowledge. How much writing we produce and consume is supposedly a measure of our learning. In fact, all schooling and learning revolves around writing. To be learned is to be published and well read. Writing dictates how we define knowledge, and how we define knowledge promotes writing. Either way, writing is the currency of our knowledge. We are hostile to any knowledge that has no foundation in the written word. In order for something to qualify as knowledge for us, meaning in order for something to be observable and measurable, we believe that something must lend for words and symbols that could be put down on paper. Thus every syllabus begins with a list of required readings, and every scholar must be ready to either publish or perish. Writing is a creature of institutions. Its hegemony has no origins in knowledge. The purpose of scholarly writing is to help the institution of schooling maintain command and control. It facilitates hierarchy. Scholarly writing allows us to exercise control over what knowledge is disseminated and consumed. It allows us to sort and rank levels of learning, as well as exercise control over the learning process. Ultimately, scholarly writing gives us the illusion of power and control. Moreover, scholarly writing is about precision. We must write with precision and conform to all the rigid conventions of scholarly writing. We must be comfortable with perceiving and experiencing the world in ways that comport with scholarly writing. We must also be willing to be institutionally obedient, as in being willing to submit to all the conventions that scholarly writing demands. We must also be comfortable with all the anxiety that comes with scholarly writing. After all, the anxiety is endless. Everything comes down to the writing. Success in academe is dependent on writing well and writing often. Our writing is constantly scrutinized and evaluated. It is all that matters. In most cases there is no regard for the subject of the writing, or why it is important. Then again, the conventions of scholarly writing make it all but impossible to write about anything that is genuinely important. The reason again being that scholarly writing is first and foremost performing an institutional and hierarchical function. In the end, all that matters is who has judged the writing to be good. Which press published your book? Which journal published your article?

But much more than our writing is being evaluated. It is we who are ultimately being evaluated and reevaluated. We use writing to measure how learned and schooled and cultured a person is. Through writing we measure pedigree. This is why we value good schooling. Presumably, good schooling makes for much learning, which in turn makes for good writing. This, again, is why the anxiety is endless. Through our writing our pedigree (or lack thereof) is always on display. By the quality of the writing we can supposedly know a person's intellectual pedigree. We continue to make believe that we are seeking to uphold the necessary standards of excellence that will make our knowledge credible. But this, again, is nothing but a pretense. We are institutionalized through scholarly writing. Without the cultivation of scholarly writing, the institution of schooling becomes vulnerable. It can potentially implode, threatening the collapse of all the other institutions that depend on schooling for legitimacy. Scholarly publishing is nothing but an ideological exercise to legitimize pedigree and reinforce the belief that life does favor the strongest, fittest, and brightest. This, again, is why schooling matters. It presumably reflects pedigree. This is also why we can never ask why the writing is important, or how does the writing enlarge or challenge how we perceive the world. Scholarly writing has nothing to do with learning. Its purpose is institutional, to remind us that our intellectual endowments are unequal and set by nature. Only a select few are supposedly the best and brightest.

Good writing supposedly means cognitive superiority, as in naturally possessing the ability to process the world rationally and computationally. This is presumably why our scholarly writing is superior. It reflects our own natural superiority. By being superiorly rational and computational, we can develop and sustain complex arguments. We can also control our emotions and passions and thereby avoid mistaking emotion for persuasion. Good scholarly writing supposedly demands objectivity. We must supposedly be capable of separating ourselves from our object of study. We can avoid becoming entangled and muddling our understanding of the subject of our writing. In other words, good scholarly writing demands self-control. We must be disciplined and avoid being seduced by our emotions and passions. All of this is what makes scholarly writing an ideological apparatus. It coercively and insidiously conforms our being to a certain way of perceiving and experiencing the world. In turn, scholarly writing reinforces a certain way of perceiving and experiencing the world. This reality reminds us that how we perceive the world is inseparable from how we communicate about the world. To change one involves changing the other. But this is also how the status quo remains the status quo. Through scholarly writing the status quo promotes an ideology that values hierarchy.

CHAPTER 3

ON METAPHORS AND KNOWLEDGE

WE USE LIGHT AS A metaphor for knowledge. To be educated is to be enlightened. To inquire is to illuminate. When we understand something it is because a light went on in our heads. The metaphor of light would have us assume that the world is of darkness. We presumably evolve by displacing darkness with light. The more light we can generate, the more knowledge we will acquire, and the less we will stumble and fumble around in the darkness. So the project of knowledge becomes a matter of how much light can we generate. What kind of devices can we design and build to generate as much light as possible? It becomes a matter of power, of trying to build more and more powerful devices that can displace more and more darkness. Without being able to generate this kind of power, we will supposedly be left in darkness.

We therefore measure our progress by how much power we are capable of generating—that is, by how much light our devices are capable of generating. We are to assume that acquiring knowledge is about shedding light. The more light we can generate, the more knowledge we will acquire. The metaphor would have us believe that there is a world outside and separate from us that is fixed and constant. By generating light we are merely revealing the workings of *this* world. The metaphor of light would therefore have us believe that there is nothing political, cultural, or historical about the project of knowledge. We presumably only generate the light that makes for the discovery of truth. Ultimately, knowledge presumably comes from our devices and instruments. The metaphor of light would have us believe that illumination involves no interpretation, and is thereby devoid of motives, biases, prejudices, ambitions, assumptions, suspicions, and all else that makes us human. This is why the metaphor of light likes the language of observation and findings. What is illuminated can presumably be observed and found by all. Knowledge becomes something that can be observed, and because we observe it we can define and measure it. Illumination becomes the measure of knowledge. Only that which we can illuminate, define, and measure qualifies as knowledge. Anything else is cast as conjecture.

What this means is that the project of knowledge is really about the quest for illumination. When illumination occurs, what is illuminated is presumably visible (observable) to all, regardless of our race, culture, and politics. Thus the goal is to generate as much illumination as possible so that our observations are visible to all and beyond dispute. That knowledge must be observable means that knowledge must have certain dimensions that favor certain senses. We must be able to see it, or be able to create the impression that we are seeing it. This is how modeling and diagramming became indispensible elements in the project of knowledge. We treat our models and diagrams as accurate reflections of reality. Thus the rise of abstract thought and ways of conceiving and perceiving things that are outside of any direct involvement in the real world, which is to say ways of conceiving and perceiving things that are devoid of all the peculiarities, complexities, ambiguities, and difficulties that come with the real world. Abstract thought is about living in our own minds, in our own worlds. We are released from all the demands, constraints, hassles, and confusions that come with the real world. Nevertheless, the fact is that abstract thought is increasingly responsible for much of our knowledge, meaning that much of our knowledge is abstract and outside of the bounds of the real world. It also means that models and diagrams are now ubiquitous in our observations and descriptions.

However, if knowledge comes from illumination, what explains our inability to replicate our observations? Such was long the best-kept secret in academe. But now the truth is out and we await a plausible account as to why we are unable to do something (replicate our observations) that is fundamental to the project of knowledge. Yet for how long have we been of the illusion that results and findings were being replicated and the project of knowledge was moving forward and illuminating nearly everything? We also continue to believe in the accuracy of our models and diagrams, even though all ecologies are inherently unpredictable because small disruptions can have seismic effects. Moreover, what of the abstract thought processes that are generating more and more knowledge of the world? How do such processes shape and influence our being and becoming? That is, what becomes of people who are increasingly divorced from a world laden with ambiguity and complexity? What kind of mind do these abstract thought processes produce? In fact, what kind of knowledge can come from a mind that functions from the level of abstraction? How can abstract thought put us in harmony with a world that has real constraints? Abstract thought makes for an abstract world, one that must ultimately be virtual so as to save us from the demands and challenges of the real world. This is the moment of history that is now upon us.

We now have unsurpassed stockpiles of knowledge, yet most of this knowledge has no relevance to anything, or at least to anything important. On the other hand, even with all this knowledge now available to us, we are more and more incapable of dealing with the demands of the real world, such as being able to recognize the limits of this world. But how else to explain the kind of knowledge that we have created that is now responsible for destroying the world? How else to explain our own indifference to this peril and the destruction that is coming from our own hands? Yet there is no indictment of our knowledge. Neither is there any indictment of how did we come to create a knowledge that could make for so much destruction. We continue to believe that science is purely in the illumination business. The problem presumably resides in how science is being used and to what ends. Nuclear technology would be a case in point. We can supposedly use this technology for either good or evil. The choice is supposedly only ours to make. But what of the hazardous waste that this technology produces that will threaten us for thousands of years? What other people have ever brought such a destructive knowledge into the world?

We are to assume that the knowledge we are creating and generating is inevitable. We are, again, merely in the illumination business. More knowledge presumably means more illumination. But before there is illumination there is the metaphor of illumination. All metaphors have ideological origins. To believe that the world requires illumination will always make for a knowledge that promises illumination. Our knowledge is doing the bidding of our metaphors, and in turn, ultimately the bidding of our ideology. To believe that we require illumination to survive and thrive is to assume the problem that faces us is the absence of illumination (darkness). We are presumably born into darkness, without the knowledge we need to survive and thrive. If we are therefore going to survive and thrive, we have to illuminate the world by our own hands. We have to conquer darkness. Darkness supposedly represents all that threatens us.

But how did we come to be afraid of the dark? Is this fear existential, universal? Possibly, we do need illumination to survive and thrive. But maybe we need a different kind of illumination, and also a different way of illuminating the world. On the other hand, maybe what we really need is a different metaphor, one that can release us from the conflict between light darkness. After all, this is a false divide as light and darkness reside within each other and also define each other. We will never, even remotely, conquer the world's darkness. What then is the value and purpose of this enterprise? Why must we continue to be afraid of the dark? Why also must we continue to believe that amassing knowledge is our way out of the darkness and ultimately integral to our prosperity? Where, after all, is the evidence that affirms any correlation between illumination and enlightenment? That is, where is the evidence that shows our increasing stockpiles of knowledge enhancing our prosperity? But such is the power of ideology. Even in the absence of evidence that illumination brings prosperity and enlightenment, we remain determined to illuminate everything, and convinced that doing so is necessary.

CHAPTER 4

ON THE COMING SINGULARITY

EXCITEMENT IS IN THE AIR. The final merging of man and machine is near. "We will soon," claims Vernor Vinge, "create intelligences greater than our own. When this happens, human history will have reached a kind of singularity, an intellectual transition as impenetrable as the knotted space-time at the center of a black hole, and the world will pass far beyond our understanding." This coming singularity will supposedly unleash all of our potentiality. We will finally exceed all the obstacles that have long dogged our progress and evolution. We might even vanquish death, as diseases will be no more. Hunger will also be a thing of the past as food will be abundant due to new breakthroughs in bioengineering.

So again, excitement is in the air. The singularity is upon us. It constitutes, according to advocates, the highest point in our evolution. This is apparently the moment we have long been waiting for. This is where history will finally end. We will enter a new world where the union between man and machine will be complete. We are to believe that the evolution of technology is on the side of nature. It is natural and good. We are to also assume that this evolution is inevitable and necessary. It must occur in order for us to continue to evolve. According to Hans Moravec of Carnegie Mellon University's Robotics Institute, "At the same time, by performing better and cheaper, the robots will displace humans from essential roles. If their capacities come to include self-replication (and why not?), they may displace us altogether. That was the pattern of our own emergence in competition with other human species, including Neanderthal man and *Homo erectus*. Personally, I am not alarmed at this; these future machines will be our progeny, our mind children, built in our image and likeness, ourselves less flawed, more potent. Like biological children of previous generations, they will embody humanity's best chances for long-term survival. It behooves us to give them every advantage and, when we have passed evolution's torch, bow out."

Without the singularity we will apparently succumb to the world's malevolent forces. We will be vanquished by epidemics and pandemics. We will run out of food and water as our numbers explode. The singularity will supposedly allow us to avoid all of these horrors by giving us the means to amass unsurpassed amounts of information. Presumably, our own progress is attributable to our own increasing capacity to amass information, which in turn improves our ability to manipulate the world to our advantage. Our evolutionary prosperity supposedly depends on our ability to successfully manipulate the world, meaning that evolution is supposedly a story of domination and manipulation through our amassing and commanding of information.

The singularity will apparently happen between 2040 and 2045. But what happens after the singularity comes and goes? That is, what happens when all the excitement comes to misery and dread? Indeed, what is all but certain is that the singularity will make for no redemption. The machines will rise at our peril. Still, the singularity is seductive. For what could be more appealing than a world without disease and death, poverty and hunger? The singularity only requires us to wait for the technology to unfold. We are merely to get out of the way and allow the process to run its natural course. We should also refrain from trying to interfere with the process, as ultimately the outcomes will supposedly be best for us. We should have no fear of what the singularity will do or make of us. Again, the singularity is merely another stage in our evolution. But to believe that such is the case is to also believe that the singularity is devoid of ideology. Nothing is devoid of ideology. Everything is shaped by our beliefs, values, fears, hopes, and experiences. The technologies that are increasingly upon us are fundamentally changing how we engage and experience the world. In many ways, these technologies are heightening our illusion of control, deepening our belief that we are actually enhancing our ability to manipulate the world. We seem increasingly convinced that our new technologies are affording us a more precise knowledge of the world. This precision is presumably giving us a superior capacity to manipulate the world, and this knowledge will save us by allowing us to control our fates. We will no longer be at the mercy of the workings of the natural world.

The western and European world has always sought a knowledge that will allow us to manipulate the world in every which way. It believes that this knowledge will make for redemption. This is why the singularity is such a significant moment. It supposedly constitutes our emancipation from the natural world. Our evolution will now be principally shaped by technological rather than biological forces. So what happens in the virtual world now becomes much more important than what happens in the natural world. Our emerging technologies will also supposedly take us into a new threshold of evolution that will unbind us from the limits of the natural and physical world. What promises to emerge, according to advocates of the singularity, is a new and superior consciousness that is free from all the speciesism and tribalism that comes with the natural world. Again, what could be more seductive than the promise of a new consciousness that will finally get us beyond the racisms, nationalisms, and fundamentalisms that have long tortured us?

This is why excitement is in the air. Our emerging technologies will also supposedly promote democracy and end tyranny. Wars will be a thing of the past as democracies presumably never go to war with each other. Indeed, Steven Pinker claims that the superiority of the western and European world can be seen in our unparalleled success in lessening and controlling our violent instincts and impulses. This is presumably why the western and European civilization is the most civilized. But this thesis requires us to forget the unparalleled murder, mayhem, and misery that happened within the western and European world during the last century. There is simply no case to be made that the singularity correlates with moral progress. Even as the singularity nears, the world teeters on the brink of nuclear armageddon, and our proclivity for war shows no sign of abating. In fact, even Charles Darwin never believed that evolution correlates with moral progress. However, this notion of moral progress is vital to understanding and legitimizing the singularity. It is responsible for much of the excitement and anticipation. What is attractive about our notion of moral progress is that it supposedly reflects our own moral progress. If we are on the cusp of the highest point in our evolution, then we are no doubt the most morally advanced. We can now justify our actions and decisions by the fact that we are morally superior. This is presumably why we have a moral obligation to impose our values on others, as well as our various institutions. This mentality can also be in our international charities and philanthropies. We seem convinced that our moral superiority gives us permission to decide and determine what is best for other peoples. We believe that the adoption of our technologies is vital for the development and moral evolution of other peoples. We reject charges that our interventions constitute a new kind of colonialism. We claim that the natives are only too eager to adopt our technologies, and are no less excited about the coming singularity. In fact, many prominent voices from non-western nations contend that only the singularity can save these nations from further peril, such as increasing food scarcity, exploding populations, and dwindling natural resources.

The singularity assumes that our redemption resides in the amassing of a certain kind of technocratic knowledge. We are to focus on developing the methodologies and technologies that will allow us to amass only this kind of knowledge. In turn, this knowledge reinforces the world we already perceive. The process becomes self-perpetuating, self-correcting, and self-legitimizing. It becomes all but impossible to stop. Our only recourse is to wait for the process to implode, as such is what happens eventually to closed systems. But what will be left in its wake, and what kind of peril will its implosion pose to us?

To assume that our redemption requires accumulating and commanding a certain kind of knowledge requires us to also believe that we are capable of extracting this kind of knowledge from the world. We are supposedly capable of unlocking the world's secrets and knowing how everything works. We will smash the atom again and again until we know everything. But the world makes plain that we are engaging in nothing but a fool's errand. We merely have to look up and recognize that billions of galaxies abound. What kind of precise knowledge can we possibly hope to acquire of such magnitude? Yet somehow we have come to possess this enormous hubris, believing that we are on the cusp of developing a theory that will explain everything. The singularity is as much hubris as illusion. But everything about the doing of science promotes hubris and illusion. That science can only allow for the pursuit of those questions that it is capable of answering ensures continuity and predictability. Our questions are always answerable, and even the answers are predictable. After all, what else is a hypothesis?

Theories and methodologies are inextricable. By dictating what questions we ask, theories also dictate how we answer these questions. This is why, as Thomas Kuhn observed long ago, science is incapable of pursuing new questions. New questions can only come from new epistemologies, which in turn can only come through the implosion of dominant epistemologies. In other words, new questions can only come from the rise of new ways of perceiving and making sense of the world. This is diversity. This is why diversity matters. The singularity is about singularizing and homogenizing. It seeks to vanquish diversity. It perceives diversity as inherently negative. Indeed, diversity and machines are incompatible. Machines require conformity and homogeneity in order to function effectively. The goal of the singularity is to use machines to make us function better, such as making us better decision-makers. In fact, the goal of the singularity is to make us better machines so we can attain superior computing and processing power. We are, after all, merely (and supposedly) survival machines. However, because we are merely survival machines, our survival is presumably dependent on being the best machines we can be, which involves maximizing our ability to absorb and process information. So the question that will always be most important to us is how can we maximize our ability to consume and analyze information? We are to believe that the singularity constitutes the rise of this moment. We must now evolve into cyborgs and become the highest expression of our evolution. So with the singularity comes the rise of the machines and our belief that machines will make everything better by allowing us to exceed our subjectivity, fallibility, and physicality. Besides increasing our physical capacity, machines will supposedly also increase our rigor, objectivity, and rationality.

In doing all of these things, machines will increase our functionality and ultimately, our prosperity. If so, however, what to make of the new headlines that claim that scientists are now increasingly afraid of the threats that our machines are posing to us?

The problem is with our bodies. The western and European world has always been repulsed by our bodies. We perceive our bodies as fallible, unreliable, and gullible. We have always sought to use technologies to improve our capabilities, as well to correct for our supposed deficiencies. So if our bodies are weak and fragile, machines must be strong and sturdy. If our bodies are susceptible to all manner of passions, emotions, and persuasions, machines are to be rational, objective, and rigorous. This is why we are increasingly relying on machines to make our decisions. We trust machines to do a better job. We believe that machines are better than us. Besides possessing much more computing power, we believe that machines are simply much more impartial, devoid of our subjectivity and gullibility. We have always sought to become different from what we perceive ourselves to be. This is how we are now becoming machines. We believe that our increasing dependence on machines is a good thing. This trend supposedly shows us becoming more rigorous and efficient. Indeed, the goal of machines is efficiency, using resources in ways that minimizes and even eliminates waste. In seeking to make us machines the goal is to maximize our efficiency. Becoming rational, mathematical, and computational supposedly makes us efficient, thereby improving the prospects of our own evolution. We are to believe that our inefficiencies supposedly come from our bodies, meaning that our bodies are responsible for the inefficiencies that impede our progress and evolution. If we are therefore going to move forward, something must apparently be done about our bodies. However, where did the notions of objectivity, rationality, and rigor come from? How did we arrive at these notions? How did we come to despise our bodies? On the other hand, is our quest to become more rational and computational making us better? Does the condition of the world reflect this improvement and betterment? Is our increasing dependence on machines making us better? If so, what again to make of the headlines of scientists warning of ecological doom? How could our improving rationality be responsible for threatening our survival?

We can no doubt be gullible, prejudiced, and lazy. But this is a problem of exercise and development, specifically the lack thereof. Being human requires work. We must struggle. Through struggle we become resilient. Through struggle we realize our capabilities and potentialities. Through struggle we evade the kinds of anxieties, insecurities, and paranoia that disfigure, cripple, and dehumanize us. Through struggle we enlarge how we perceive and experience the world. In sum, through struggle we become human by enlarging our capacity to imagine, to innovate, to believe, to forgive, to empathize, and to love. In changing our relation to ourselves, struggle changes our relation to the world, as well as our perception of the world. Through struggle we come to a more positive and constructive view of the world. We recognize the need for grace and humility. We will never achieve a complete and absolute understanding of anything. We must always be learning.

To struggle is to come to terms with the fact that what is unknown will always exceed what is known. The world requires us to struggle, to even recognize that struggle makes us better. This is why the singularity poses such a threat to us. It promises to release us from the need to struggle by giving us the answers and solutions to everything. We will supposedly know all the world's secrets. Nothing will be a mystery. We will have the end of ambiguity as our actions and decisions will now be based on our newfound ability to analyze every possible outcome. However, in seeking to save us from the world's mystery and ambiguity, the singularity impoverishes our humanity by impeding the struggle that is necessary to become human. Our bodies become disfigured and crippled by the anxieties, insecurities, and paranoia that result from a lack of struggle. Thus, as the singularity nears, the astonishing rise in all kinds of neuroses and psychoses is hard to miss. Our anxieties, insecurities, and paranoia are tormenting us to the hilt. But the singularity being the singularity, promises a medical fix, one that will supposedly be perfect, easy, and final. Thus our neuroses and psychoses are increasingly medicalized and pharmaceuticalized. Take a pill and be happy. Such again is the seductive nature of the singularity. Our redemption requires nothing much from us. The solution to our misery can supposedly be found in technology. However, what to make now of the fact that the medications and prescriptions are worsening and compounding our neuroses and psychoses? Our technology fix is proving to be no fix at all. However, who really wants to struggle when the singularity continues to be so seductive? On the other hand, as we become increasingly tortured by our anxieties, insecurities, and paranoia, how we perceive and relate to the world will reflect this misery and torment. The ugly we perceive in ourselves becomes the ugly we perceive in the world. All of this ugly will make us do ugly things. This is why the singularity promises nothing good.

Even with the aid of every possible kind of technology, we will never achieve the rationality and objectivity that is supposedly necessary for our survival and prosperity. The singularity is based on nothing but an illusion. For what case is to be made that our problems result from a lack of rationality and objectivity? Both are ideological constructs, laden with all of our own fears, beliefs, and prejudices. There are no definitions of rationality and objectivity that stand outside of time and space. Moreover, there is no case to be made that the evolution of technology correlates with moral progress. Again, if there is such a correlation, why all the fears from prominent scientists about our impending doom? How could moral progress make for our demise? But what is so deficient about what human beings can do that no technology will ever do, like the ability to imagine, to empathize, to hope, to believe, and to love? Why are these attributes incapable of ensuring our prosperity? In fact, why are we willing to believe that these attributes are lacking, and that we are lacking? Apparently, all that is wrong with us can be found in our mortality. We grow old and feeble and then die. Our life span is barely significant. Even most trees outlive us. The goal of the singularity is to conquer our mortality. It views our mortality as a defect, as a problem that needs addressing, as the next matter that needs evolutionary attention. But is our mortality really a flaw that needs an evolutionary fix? Would this fix enrich our prosperity and extend our functionality? In short, should the conquering of our mortality be our ambition?

We no doubt seem to have an existential fear of death. We like conformity, stability, and predictability. Change brings anxiety, especially when the change is immediate and seismic. Yet change is also inevitable. But our fear of death touches and influences many things. Besides affecting how we perceive and experience change, this fear also affects how we relate and communicate with each other, as well as how we relate to and perceive the world. In many ways, this fear just about influences everything. But this is by no means constant. We all experience this fear of death differently. Ideology shapes how we experience this fear. We can experience this fear negatively or positively, deeply or otherwise. There is simply no natural law dictating how we experience and make sense of our own mortality. History, however, reveals that how we engage with this fear of death has enormous consequences. To be hostile to this fear makes us hostile to change. We encourage and promote only those things that sustain the status quo. We are also much more averse to exploring and learning new things. Diversity, flexibility, and spontaneity are problems for us. We need customs and traditions to help us find and maintain meaning. Even the possibility of chaos torments us. We are obsessed with order and looking to the past for direction. Trust is also a problem for us. In fact, anything that requires risk and vulnerability heightens our anxiety. Empathy and compassion are problems for us; as to look at the world from the perspective of others involves risk and vulnerability, such as our own truth being wrong. We may have to change, which means that something may have to die. In all things, our own self-interest matters most, as self-interest also means self-preservation. However, without death we are incapable of being born anew. Being afraid of our own mortality impedes all that we are capable of being and becoming. Harboring such fear makes us susceptible to all the things that disfigure our humanity. But we can have a different relation to death.

We can embrace death. Embracing death pushes us to live honestly, passionately, and courageously, and deepens what we are capable of perceiving and experiencing. To embrace our mortality is to embrace all of life's ambiguity and mystery. We lose the impulse to impose our truths on others and have the world conform and submit to our fears. We are willing to look at the world in new ways because we have no fear of relinquishing our truths. We have the courage to be vulnerable. To embrace our mortality also organically detaches us from everything. It realigns our relation to the world. We give back to the world its wonder and mystery. We in turn acquire a newfound humility that keeps us vulnerable to possibility.

To look closely at the human experience is to understand the ravages of attachment. Attachment means being unable to release ourselves from all that we believe and value. Our creations become our gods. All of the world's great religions warn us about worshipping false gods. But such is the problem with the singularity. It is determined to impose a singular reality on us. We are to believe that this vision is best for us. Technology will save us from all that is wrong and deficient about us. Escaping the singularity is now all but impossible. It increasingly intrudes upon everything, insidiously vanquishing other worldviews. All of the world is now texting, tweeting, and facebooking. The singularity is achieving a universality and homogeneity that even religion never came close to achieving. Its hold on us is now all but impossible to dislodge. Even fathoming a world without the singularity is challenging. In fact, even criticisms of the singularity never rise to the level of unplugging our machines or challenging the singularity's bedrock assumptions. The singularity constitutes the highest level of attachment—being attached to something that permeates and influences every manner of our being. For who can now imagine a world without machines? The singularity becomes our only vision of the world, or at least the only vision we perceive as viable. We are all complicit in the making of this situation. We are seduced by the singularity. But the singularity is still about promoting attachment, vanquishing the world's diversity, and bringing us under a singular consciousness. Never before has the world seen this kind of homogeneity or even sought to achieve this kind of singularity. But this is supposed to be progress. This is supposed to be the highest point in our evolution, the making of a singular consciousness.

We are now on the cusp of breaking completely from the world's natural order. The singularity assumes that our redemption resides in homogeneity. But the natural world reveals that our redemption resides in diversity. No doubt, the order of the natural world will ultimately prevail. In such ways the world is truly just. The homogeneity that the singularity promotes will eventually make for its demise. Still, how did we become so divorced and separated from the natural world? How did we come to believe that our violation of the world's natural order would go without consequences? But in this way the singularity was inevitable. Being hostile to ourselves made us hostile to the world. When we began to distance and separate ourselves from our bodies we also began to distance and separate ourselves from the world. The separating and distancing was from the rise of the anxieties that made it difficult to embrace our bodies. However, separation from our bodies also means separation from our minds. This is why our theories have such an inherent hostility to our bodies. This is also why we have these elaborate methodologies in our sciences to remove and discipline the body. Our distrust and suspicion of the body runs deep. However, the more we separate and distance ourselves from our bodies, the more our bodies torment and anguish us. Such is the order of the singularity. Born out of our hostility to our bodies, the singularity is laden with all the anxieties that estrange and alienate us from our bodies. As such, the singularity is also laden with all the anxieties that estrange and alienate us from the world.

That we can strive in homogeneity is plainly false. We merely have to look at history to understand the ravages of homogeneity. But homogeneity is much more than merely false. It is an illusion, just like the illusion that we can separate our bodies from how we perceive and make sense of things, and just like the illusion that we can separate our fate from the fate of the natural world. But even the best illusions are nothing but illusions, and will eventually implode. Such implosion awaits the singularity. However, we continue to believe that homogeneity is necessary for our prosperity. This is why we demand that immigrants linguistically and culturally assimilate. It is also why we believe on sharing a common set of norms about what is decent and civil. Even our popular theories of diversity value homogeneity over diversity. The purpose of the singularity is to promote homogeneity. It showcases our determination to achieve the highest levels of homogeneity. Indeed, homogeneity appeals to our most primal instincts and impulses. We should supposedly be safe and secure amongst those we perceive as being like us. Homogeneity is also easy. It involves hardly any risk or effort. It also promises stability and continuity, saving us from the anxiety that comes with ambiguity and diversity. Finally, homogeneity is existentially appealing. Our own well-being, and those of our kind, should be first and foremost. Supposedly, without love of self, including love of our own kind, there can be no love of others. We are seemingly existentially inclined to love ourselves and our kin and kind first. However, besides being ecologically destructive, homogeneity promotes narcissism, which in turn is the root of all racisms, nationalisms, ethnocentrisms, and fundamentalisms. Focus on self invariably makes for obsession with self. Narcissism impedes our ability to learn from others, to make new relationships that could possibly offer new resources for growth and development. Existentially, homogeneity creates a false notion of self and personhood. Concern for self is inseparable from concern for others. Our humanity resides in our relationships. Our relational resources shape who and what we become. Epistemologically, homogeneity impedes knowledge by confining us to people who look at the world like we do.

This is why science has no capacity to ask new questions. However, without being able to ask new questions, what becomes of our prosperity? How could any species evolve successfully without being able to learn? But such is the irony of the singularity. It supposedly represents the culmination of our learning, the moment where our sciences will allow us to know everything and do almost anything. Instead, the singularity represents a profound ignorance. For how else do we account for our pending ecological doom as a result of our own doing? What other species has shown such ignorance? Yet the singularity would have us believe that our ecological problem has nothing to do with the nature of our knowledge. It comes from how we have decided to use our knowledge. The common analogy is guns. It is supposedly human beings rather than guns who kill. However, guns give us the ability to kill in ways that are different to other ways of killing. Guns allow us to kill abstractly. In other words, guns change how we perceive and experience killing, which in turn changes how we make decisions about killing. The singularity is also changing how we perceive and experience the world. It divorces us from ourselves, each other, and the world. No doubt, the singularity has achieved an unsurpassed capacity to acquire and disseminate information quickly and efficiently. Our stockpiles of information are vast. But how much of this information is actually valuable is a different matter. Most of this information has nothing to do with anything. Because we are estranged and alienated from ourselves and each other, our knowledge is also estranged and alienated from the world. In being born out of our own separation and alienation, our knowledge has nothing to do with us and what matters to us. For instance, communication theory makes no mention of love, mercy, grace, compassion, tenderness, and forgiveness. Yet how could any knowledge of communication be devoid of these notions and still be valuable to us? On the other hand, our knowledge of communication is vast. We can fill rooms with our scholarly books and articles. Conferences are also endless. However, with all this knowledge of communication, never before have we been so isolated and separated from each other. So again, how much of our knowledge is valuable? That is, valuable in terms of expanding what we are capable of perceiving, understanding, and being. Valuable in terms of making for a world with less misery and suffering. Valuable in terms of making our lives more meaningful.

The singularity believes that the body should play no role in how we acquire and adjudicate knowledge. We should strive to limit its influence. Its presence and influence supposedly compromise the objectivity that is the measure of a true and reliable knowledge. Thus the singularity employs an array of strategies, methodologies, and technologies to remove the body's influence. But objectivity is nothing but an illusion, a creation of our own alienation. In order to acquire a valuable knowledge we have to engage knowledge as complete human beings. We must strive to be completely vulnerable. This means dealing with questions like, why are we asking the questions we are asking? Why do these questions matter to us? Or, why do these questions appeal to us? What are these questions asking us to believe, and why are we inclined to believe and value these things? How do these questions promise to save our lives? The singularity would have us believe that our redemption resides in our ability to acquire a knowledge that will allow us to dominate and manipulate the world. The more of this knowledge we can acquire, the more control we will supposedly have over our destiny. The singularity would have us believe that we are achieving this outcome and thereby achieving dominion over the world. But of course reality tells a different story. Maybe our redemption has nothing much to do with acquiring anything. Maybe our redemption resides in being rather than knowing, or in the promotion of a kind of being that promotes a certain kind of knowing. In other words, maybe our redemption resides in enlarging and deepening our modes of being rather acquiring anything.

Teaching can inspire, challenge, and even seduce. But even the best teaching cannot make anyone learn anything. Learning requires courage, and that courage can only come from us. Moreover, as most of the knowledge that the singularity aspires to disseminate is anything but valuable, finding a reason to learn this knowledge becomes a challenge. But with the need to acquire and disseminate this knowledge effectively and efficiently comes the need for all kinds of institutions, such as schools, colleges, scholarly associations, foundations, professional organizations, and publishers. The process becomes institutionalized and bureaucratized. Diversity becomes intolerable and impossible. With any kind of institution, conformity is the status quo. No institution thrives by encouraging diversity. However, when knowledge becomes institutionalized and bureaucratized, we also become institutionalized and bureaucratized. The demands of conformity impede our ability to imagine the world in new ways. We also never develop any faith and trust in our ability to ask really important questions. All that we can do and have permission to do is ask questions that we are capable of answering, which means that we can only use those theories and methodologies that are available to us, which in turn means that we will produce no knowledge that threatens the status quo.

Still, the singularity claims to oppose institutions and bureaucracy. It rails against how both stifle innovation by imposing all kinds of rules and regulations. But in reality the singularity is making for an institutionalization that is unsurpassed. Machines have the lowest threshold for diversity. Machines need conformity in terms of specifications and regulations in order to function properly, especially when connected to other machines. If institutions can have a certain amount of variability, machines when integrated with other machines can barely have any. The singularity is literally a singularity. The fact that the world's linguistic diversity is disappearing as the singularity unfolds is by no means a random association. That the world is becoming increasingly globalized and homogenized as the singularity nears is also by no means a random association. The singularity is always conspiring against diversity. It intuitively knows that diversity is its greatest threat. On the other hand, never before has diversity faced such as a threat as the singularity. In no realm is diversity safe.

Diversity is the canary in the mine. To lose diversity is to lose everything. Besides losing the ability to perceive and experience the world in new ways, the end of diversity also means the end of learning. It also means the end of empathy and compassion. In this way, the end of diversity also means that narcissism abounds. We are obsessed with only our own self-interest. The end of diversity also means the end of vulnerability, as in our willingness to be open and honest with each other, especially with those we narrowly perceive to be different. We are inclined to perceive others as foes rather than friends. The end of diversity also means the end of communication. For without empathy and compassion, communication is impossible. Without communication, we lose the ability to demystify each other's differences. We also lose the ability to form deep relationships. Isolation rules, as well as all the attending neuroses and psychoses. Ultimately, the loss of diversity means the loss of possibility, as in the possibility to learn new things, to make new friends, to form new kinds of relationships, to access new resources, and to grow and become better human beings.

The loss of diversity diminishes our humanity. It makes us less human. Diversity comes into the world through our moral evolution. It cannot be contrived or manufactured for the sake of social and political expediency. But this is all the singularity can give us, a contrived and manufactured version of diversity. Diversity is presumably about differences, but only those that we are capable of tolerating, assimilating, and bridging—that is, only those that pose no threat to the status quo. Anything else we condemn, punish, and banish. But how could diversity be defined by our own moral standards? If such is the case, or should be the case, then every prophet deserved to be persecuted for violating our moral and ideological norms. Evidently, diversity must be something different. It must possess the capacity to disrupt the order of things in ways that stretch our humanity. Diversity should bring out the best in us. This is how the singularity impedes diversity. The singularity thrives through homogeneity. It is inherently incapable of promoting anything that can disrupt the status quo. In other words, the singularity has no inherent capacity to produce prophets.

CHAPTER 5

On Modern Philosophy

It is all Descartes's fault. It was Rene Descartes, the father of modern philosophy and analytical geometry, who famously said, "I think, therefore I am." This is the defining statement of the western/European world. Descartes never said, "We think, therefore we are." Instead, the focus is on "I," like the "I" in individualism. For Descartes, being human begins and ends with "I." "I think, therefore I am." Being human is about what "I" do. For Descartes, there is no "Us" or "We" in being human. Being human is supposedly an individual thing. There is nothing relational, communal, or ecological about being human for Descartes. "I think, therefore I am." "I am" is all that matters. Others should look out for themselves, do what is best for themselves. "I" will look out for myself. "I" will do what is best for me. "I am" the captain of my destiny, master of my fate.

Moreover, for Descartes, being human is fundamentally about our capacity to think. "I think, therefore I am." Descartes never said, "I love, therefore I am." Or, "I empathize, therefore I am." Or, "I share, therefore I am." Or, "I forgive, therefore I am." Or, "I care therefore I am." For Descartes, the measure of our humanity is found in our capacity to think. How much we are capable of thinking will determine what we become. Thus the western/European world continues to devote enormous resources to measuring and expanding our ability to think. Every standardized test was born of this legacy. It is also why we continue to use these tests to organize and allocate power and resources. We believe that these tests can reliably measure the limits of our humanity, which of course assumes that our potentiality can be measured and quantified.

Descartes is responsible for our obsession with mind. Besides being responsible for our obsession with measuring and identifying our minds, Descartes is also responsible for our obsession with finding techniques to develop the mind. If, after all, the mind is responsible for thinking, that process which supposedly defines the human experience, then attending to the mind must be our first concern. For what becomes of our mind will supposedly determine what becomes of us. Descartes is therefore also responsible for the division between mind and body, as well as our neglect of the latter. In fact, Descartes is responsible for deepening our suspicion of the body by encouraging us to believe that the body, with all its supposedly unruly desires, impulses, instincts, and passions, impedes the development of the mind. The body presumably undermines our capacity to be rational, logical, and computational. It impedes rigor, reason, and objectivity. Simply put, the body stands in the way of the rise of all that is good and necessary for our survival and prosperity. Descartes is therefore also responsible for our continuing hostility against the body and our continuing anxiety over the body.

But what have we achieved from believing Descartes? Did all our efforts to develop our minds make for a world with less misery and peril? If so, how to explain the unsurpassed horrors of the twentieth century within the western/European world? How also to explain the ecological destruction? What to make of any civilization that is responsible for so much horror and destruction? Of course, those who believe Descartes would claim that the problem is with us. We have put our knowledge to destructive ends. Apparently, our knowledge is free of ideology, devoid of biases and prejudices—that is, devoid of the body. Our knowledge is a product of rational and analytical processes. But this is a myth, an illusion, even an abomination. How could the mind be outside and separate from the body? That mind is inherently metaphorical shows well that such separation is illusory.

Metaphors reflect our subjectivity. Metaphors are ideological statements, reflecting our fears, values, beliefs, and so forth. That language is inherently metaphorical means that no observation or description of anything is devoid of our values, beliefs, fears, suspicions, ambitions, and so forth. Our metaphors shape how we perceive and make sense of things. In this way, our metaphors reflect our understanding of what the world is and should be. Metaphors create as well as describe our world. Our metaphors are ourselves. When we speak about the "hard" and "soft" sciences, that is us and what we want our knowledge to be. Changing our metaphors involves changing ourselves. In fact, no change is possible without changing our metaphors. Such is the power of metaphors. In shaping what we perceive, metaphors also shape what we imagine. So metaphors are important. Every observation and description is nothing but an interpretation, an expression of our own imagination. We can only perceive what we can imagine.

Because body and mind are bound up with each other, to be hostile to the body is to be hostile to the mind, and to terrorize the body is to terrorize the mind. So what did our hostility to the body, as a result of Descartes' urging, do to us? What does being hostile to the body do to how we perceive and experience the world? How would our metaphors have been different without this continuing hostility? Would war be still our most dominant metaphor? In fact, how would our knowledge be different, and thus our world be different? There is no doubt a relationship between the knowledge we value and prize and all the horror and carnage we have brought into the world. After all, war is the most popular metaphor in the western/European world. Nearly every tension we perceive as a duel between benevolent and malevolent forces. We aspire to produce a knowledge that will help us vanquish the latter. But in order to achieve this knowledge, we have to wage war on the body. Without doing so, objectivity would apparently be impossible. The body's passions and impulses would run rampant. Abstract thought would be impossible, resulting in a knowledge devoid of such. But when did abstract thought become a good thing? That is, when did the development of cognitive processes that are separated from reality become a good thing? What exactly is the value of abstract thought? Who lives in an abstract world? Why would any person want to live in such a world?

We achieve abstract thought by separating ourselves from our bodies, or at least promoting and reifying the illusion of doing so. It is the hallmark of such separation. The mind is finally released from the body. We have achieved abstract thought. However, releasing ourselves of the struggle between mind and body makes for a different knowledge of the world. The body is a living entity. It evolves and changes. It can be anguished, frustrated, confused, excited, and agitated. It has all kinds of dimensions. It can be domesticated and institutionalized, liberated and emancipated. It can hate and love, make war or peace. It can bleed and suffer, perish and wither. Most of all, the body believes. It can be gullible. But the body is also capable of believing the most extraordinary of things. What we believe shapes what we are capable of imagining and ultimately becoming. Indeed, nothing is more important in determining what we become than what we believe and are willing to believe. If anything, a more heuristic phrase would be, "We believe, therefore we are." We all believe something. To believe is the core of the human experience. There is no thinking without believing. In fact, no amount of thinking can rid us of the need to believe in something—that is, to cling to something that we will never be able to prove. This is why Descartes was wrong in locating our humanity in our capacity to think. This is also why we are wrong in continuing to abide by Descartes. He, again, would have us believe that our redemption resides in developing our capacity to think, or through building our minds. But how we think and what we think about all begin in what we believe.

Yet we continue to deny the fact that we believe. We disparage and ridicule persons who profess to believe. Supposedly, believing is for the weak and for those who have no appreciation of rigor and objectivity. It characterizes primitive and backward cultures, those who supposedly lack the capacity to produce reliable truths and elaborate theories. But what of our own unwillingness to recognize and acknowledge our own believing? What of our own determination to develop our minds through vast curriculums that have no recognition of the role of the body in the making of our minds? After all, what becomes of our minds will depend on what is in our hearts and souls. What we believe will shape what we perceive and experience. However, what curriculums focus on enlarging what we believe? We of course despise the fact that we believe. Believing makes us vulnerable. We like pretending that we believe nothing. We have facts. But such illusions are for fools. We need a new relation to the body as well as a new conception of mind. We need a relation that finally ends the separation between mind and body. Yes, to believe makes us vulnerable. However, without vulnerability, being able to perceive and experience the world in new ways would be impossible. Vulnerability means humility. We are of a world laden with ambiguity and mystery. We are simply devoid of any means of lessening either, and have no way of even knowing whether doing so is important. Vulnerability means that knowing matters much less than being. For again, in a world laden with ambiguity and mystery, what can we really know? Ending the illusory separation between mind and body also means recognizing and ending the illusory separation between knowing and being. Every kind of knowing makes for a certain kind of being. Looking at being in terms of vulnerability merely constitutes a different way of defining and experiencing knowing. However, because the separation between mind and body was always illusory, our ways of knowing have always been shaping our manners of being in ways that put us in conflict with the world and ourselves. All of this can be seen in our increasing misery and isolation. Being in terms of vulnerability is about how we relate, perceive, and experience the world, each other, and ourselves. Whether we experience the world as outside and separate from us is a question about being. Matters of race, gender, ethnicity, nationality, disability, and sexual orientation also deal with being. How do these concepts shape how we experience ourselves and each other? Moreover, what modes of being give rise to these concepts? Also, what modes of being give rise to the separation of theory and praxis, or that between physics, biology, mathematics, psychology, and sociology, and who is best served by these separations?

CHAPTER 6

ON THE NATURE OF THEORY

How we commonly define and experience knowledge undermines thinking. It is why we continue to mistake being educated for being learned, instruction for education, and theory for knowledge.

Thinking should challenge us to look at the consequences that come with different actions. Indeed, thinking requires courage, as in the courage to imagine the world in new ways. For no problem is ever about one thing, or two, or three. To invoke one thing as the cause of a problem reflects weakness and a lack of moral imagination. For again, no problem is ever one thing, or two, or three. Everything is intertwined. Nothing is never what it seems. There is always the possibility of a different interpretation. This, in fact, is what diversity means. It means opposing forces and structures that want to reduce the complexity of things. Herein resides the problem with feminist theory, critical race theory, queer theory, and even postcolonial theory. There is an absence of complexity, an absence of diversity. We merely have the illusion—the abstraction—that these theories are coming from a place that is about diversity.

We need to look again at how we do theory. What kind of descriptions can we offer of something when we are outside and separate from that something? How adequate can our descriptions be? This is what happens when we undermine thinking. All we can do is describe and theorize. We can neither imagine nor inspire. So rather than promoting action, we get dense and abstract descriptions, and barely any that are worth anything. We become further and further separated from the world. As the separation increases, so too does the alienation. This is why as we devise more and more elaborate and exotic theories, we seem to know less and less about less and less. There is no illumination of us. As we profess to know more and more, we become less and less. This is what happens when we conspire against thinking. We impede our ability to act upon the world by undermining the courage necessary to do so. Thinking is a way of being. It changes our relation to the world, each other, and ourselves. It removes any divide between us and the world. This is what makes thinking an insurgent undertaking. It promotes action.

The thinking person knows that we are always implicated in the affairs of the world. We are never completely absolved from what is happening in different places around the world. The fallout eventually comes our way. So thinking expands our consciousness and enlarges how we perceive and experience the world by changing our relation to everything. It has nothing to do with how many books we read or how many papers and books we write. Neither does thinking have anything to do with how much time we spend in classrooms or how many degrees we accumulate. There is probably no other place more hostile to thinking than academe. In fact, how we do all our schooling and learning impedes thinking. For where are the spaces of exploration, contemplation, and imagination? Where are the spaces for problem solving? Where are the consequences that come with thinking? Our elaborate curriculums and syllabi make sure that no such places and consequences exist. Then there are the endless departments and bureaucratized disciplines that make it all but impossible to perceive the world in new ways. Finally, there are the pedagogies and epistemologies that promote separation and alienation by assuming that knowledge is out there in the world, and being knowledgeable is about being able to acquire and manipulate this knowledge. Academe, in every way, conspires against thinking. Thus, instead of cultivating experiences that enlarge our sense of being, academe does the opposite. It infantilizes us by making us believe that by merely acquiring knowledge we can become wise. In this way, academe diminishes what being wise means and involves.

Being wise begins with recognizing that our fates are intertwined. We achieve wisdom by bringing our mind and body into communion with each other. It is this lack of separation and alienation that separates a person who is wise from one who is merely knowledgeable. With wisdom, there is never perception without compassion, understanding without grace, theory without possibility. There is always communion. For truth is never outside or separate from the body. Neither is truth ever outside of history, which means that no truth is amoral. We realize and experience truth by how large we can open our minds, hearts, and souls.

There is nothing in how we do knowledge that acknowledges this need to attend to the soul, the heart, the body. There is no doubt a persistence to the absence that promises to be enduring. We need much more than a new enterprise of knowledge. We need, ultimately, a new understanding of what being human means. For how much longer will the world put up with our juvenile self-indulgence? How much longer before the worst comes to pass? Regardless of what we choose to believe, there is still an order to this world, and such will always be the case.

CHAPTER 7
On War and Peace

BOTH LIBERALS AND CONSERVATIVES APPLAUDED the President's Nobel Peace Laureate acceptance remarks in Oslo. He was praised for being realistic, pragmatic, and most of all, patriotic. Even foes said that the President's remarks were "sober, serious, and scholarly." The President said that he could not be guided by only the examples of Martin Luther King and Gandhi. "I face the world as it is, and cannot stand idle in the face of threats to the American people. For make no mistake: Evil does exist in the world. A non-violent movement could not have halted Hitler's armies. Negotiations cannot convince al Qaeda's leaders to lay down their arms. To say that force may sometimes be necessary is not a call to cynicism—it is a recognition of history; the imperfections of man and the limits of reason."

But this is a false dichotomy, as being committed to peace has nothing to do with standing idly by as peril looms. This dichotomy distorts and trivializes what promoting peace involves. It makes believe, although the President of the United States professes to know better, that there is weakness and naiveté in the lives and creed of King and Gandhi. Presumably, persons involved in promoting peace believe that evil is merely an illusion and a non-violent movement could have put an end to the likes of Hitler and al Qaeda. Our naiveté can also be supposedly seen in our apparent failure to recognize the harsh truths of history, our imperfect nature, and "the limits of reason." But which proponent of peace is so naïve? The President gives us no names, points to no examples.

To promote peace is to oppose violence, especially the everyday and ordinary violent practices that ultimately give rise to all manner of racism and terrorism that makes war inevitable. War is an ultimate outcome. The mission of the peace movement is to end all the practices and conditions that cultivate and legitimize violence. Without violence, war is impossible. To cast peace as the negation of war is fundamentally misleading as doing so fosters the impression that peace is the absence of war. But of course this is false as slavery, apartheid, and the Holocaust all occurred in places where war was absent. To promote peace is to cultivate practices and conditions that undermine the possibility of violence. Without violence, war is impossible.

For proponents of peace, the harsh truth of history is that violence makes war inevitable. We lessen the possibility of war by impeding the conditions that promote violence. There is no such thing as a morally just war. To accept the premise of a just war is to mask all of the violence that ultimately makes war possible. For proponents of peace, this is the height of naiveté. No less naïve is believing that in a world increasingly laden with nuclear weapons, any war, regardless of however just and moral, is winnable and even survivable. Still, the President claims that "the plain fact is this: The United States of America has helped underwrite global security for more than six decades with the blood of our citizens and the strength of our arms . . . .We have done so out of enlightened self-interest—because we seek a better future for our children and grandchildren, and we believe that their lives will be better if others' children and grandchildren can live in freedom and prosperity." Indeed, such sacrifices should be duly noted. But what about the terrorism that the United States is also responsible for by toppling legitimate governments around the world, propping up cruel and murderous dictators, and proliferating all kinds of weapon systems and hardware that heighten local conflicts? What also of our reckless plundering of the world's natural resources and the attending ecological destruction that now puts the planet in peril? Who is naïve to believe that all of this violence begets no violence?

But, of course, the President makes no mention of our own culpability in burdening the world with war, misery, and peril, nor anything about our violent subjugation and oppression of African Americans and Native Americans.

We have merely made "mistakes." According to President, "our challenge" is to reconcile "two seemingly irreconcilable truths—that war is sometimes necessary, and war at some level is an expression of human folly." But this is another false schism, as war will always reflect a lack of moral imagination. This reality is amply seen in the fact that any future war involving nuclear weapons, regardless again of however just and moral, will most likely vanquish us all. What then is the value of planning and resourcing for such a war?

We can embrace other challenges. We can challenge ourselves to remove all the practices and conditions that promote and legitimize violence. These challenges require much more than simply adhering to international standards governing the use of force. For proponents of peace, there are no illusions about our capacity and even proclivity for evil. The challenge is removing all the ideological, social, and material conditions that excite, encourage, and legitimize violence, such as ending our own incarceration of so many peoples for non-violent offenses, lessening the growing gap between rich and poor, ending poverty and despair, reconfiguring our relation to the planet so as to lessen our impact, exposing the futility of punishment and retribution, encouraging self-determination for all peoples, releasing peoples from the structures and forces of imperialism and colonialism, fostering cooperation and mutuality between different peoples, and doing everything to lessen the threat and suspicion of our differences.

We understand well the case for just war, and the anguish that comes with supporting such wars. But no war, regardless of our capacity and proclivity for evil, evolves out of a material, ideological, and epistemological vacuum. This, for us, is "a plain fact" and "a hard truth." We oppose violence because we recognize only too well our abundant and stubborn capacity to wage war, but on the other hand, we also recognize that peace rather than violence will always constitute a more constructive path to our survival and prosperity.

CHAPTER 8

ON THE LIMITS OF EDUCATION

WE STILL CONTINUE TO VIEW knowledge as something that is outside and separate from being. Teaching is supposedly about helping students acquire as much of this knowledge as possible, and learning is supposedly about absorbing as much of this knowledge as possible. This is how teaching becomes reduced to "measurable learning outcomes." This is how syllabuses become laden with all kinds of instructions, regulations, and proscriptions. Behind our common way of defining and approaching teaching is a conception of knowledge that assumes that knowledge is an entity separate and outside of us. In other words, behind this common view of teaching is a belief that knowledge is a commodity we can share, acquire, and even impose. It merely depends on what techniques we use to help students absorb this knowledge.

When you enter academe there is so much you assume. You assume that academe is a place of enlightenment. It is where you come to acquire knowledge and become knowledgeable. You also assume that academe is committed to creating and generating knowledge, and through such processes will come civility and progress. But then you begin to realize that academe is hostile to knowledge. It impedes our ability to learn by refusing to allow us to take responsibility for our own learning, which means allowing us to form our own knowledge of the world on our own terms. Then you begin to realize that most of the theories and methodologies you must learn and command have nothing to do with knowledge. These theories and methodologies are really tools of ideologies, and seek to perpetuate these ideologies. Then you begin to realize that academe does nothing to promote enlightenment. Most of the knowledge that is being created, generated, and applauded means nothing and can do nothing.

The supposed divide between theory and praxis is an academic invention to come to peace with the fact that so much of the knowledge of academe is infertile. The supposed standards of academic excellence that scholars brandish are purely arbitrary, nothing but ideological artifacts. After all, how could any knowledge be judged to be excellent that in no way enlarges our view of the world, or even our understanding of what is possible? What also does it mean that such infertile knowledge is the norm of academe? That is, what does it mean that this is the kind of knowledge that academe strives to produce? Indeed, most revealing is the fact that most of this knowledge is actually never read by academics. It is the final indictment that such knowledge is completely infertile, and all the processes that create this knowledge no less so. Such is the status quo in academe. Yet why does this situation continue to be?

The problem probably begins with our believing that the world is separate and outside of us, just as much as we continue to believe that we are outside and separate from each other. Of course, what we believe is also about what we need to believe. Either way, to believe that we are outside of the world is simply false. Whatever we do to the world eventually falls back on us. Our fates are intertwined. It would seem that this should be obvious. But the status quo in academe continues to believe otherwise, even as the dire consequences of doing so can hardly be more apparent. But this again is only the beginning. Academe is about promoting and instilling this belief. We promote this belief by making believe that this knowledge is separate and outside of us. We promote this belief by making believe that learning has nothing to do with being. We assume that knowledge has nothing to do with affairs of the heart, soul, and body. After all, if knowledge is supposedly separate and outside of the body, how could the acquisition of knowledge have anything to do with the body? In other words, what could the body possibly do about the facts that objects fall to the ground, or the earth revolves around the sun? The body can supposedly do nothing about these supposed truths. Thus there is supposedly no need to attend to the body in matters of knowledge.

But human beings in no way deal with merely facts and truths. We deal in narratives, and all narratives have supposed truths and facts. All narratives also have superstitions, illusions, distortions, and even fabrications. For what is truth? It is an observation that reflects a certain way of perceiving the world. However, the body plays a vital role in shaping what we believe, perceive, and value. It does so by influencing what we are ready and willing to believe. For what we perceive, observe, and value begins with what we are ready and willing to believe. The fact that human beings deal in narratives makes plain that the body matters. It is also made obvious by the fact that every knowledge enterprise is laden with metaphors. Metaphors mediate our relation to the world and each other. Yet there are no metaphors that simply fall from the sky. Metaphors come from us. We are inherently metaphorical beings. Metaphors define everything. But this is also how we continue to make believe that the world is separate and outside of us. We deny the reality of metaphors, even when metaphors seem impossible to miss, as when we profess to being only interested in *cold* facts and *hard* truths. But this is what we continue to do in academe. We continue to make believe that knowledge is about facts and truths, and that being knowledgeable is about being able to determine fact from fiction, truth from falsehood. This is why technology now pervades academe. Facts and truths can be technologized and fetishized. We can have the illusion of the body having nothing to do with knowledge.

But narratives commit us to a different story of the human experience. We cannot teach stories the way we teach theories and methodologies. There is never one story of anything, and no story will ever lend for one interpretation, one meaning, one truth. Every story lends for another story, and another. To come to teaching from a narrative perspective is to struggle with questions like, what are these stories asking us to believe, assume, imagine? What fears, anxieties, insecurities, and paranoia come with these stories? What are the consequences and implications that come with these stories? Why do various stories appeal to us? How do these stories influence what we perceive and experience? Every story, in giving us a way to make sense of the world, simultaneously impedes our ability to imagine, perceive, and experience the world in other ways, especially in ways that are contrary to our own.

In academe we profess to being committed to promoting diversity, valuing diversity, celebrating diversity, but yet we remain hostile to any story that is contrary to our own. We ridicule and marginalize these stories. When possible we even conspire to erase these stories. We will only tolerate one story of diversity—diversity is about race, gender, disability, and sexuality. But what really matters is why do we believe this story? What does this story reveal about what we are ready to imagine and experience? Also, what does this story reveal about what we are willing to value? That our common story of diversity really constitutes no story of diversity means that our story of the world lends for no compelling understanding of the human experience. This, of course, begs the question, why? Why is our story of the world failing to lend for a much more compelling conception of diversity? What about what we believe, and need to believe, is making this impossible? Why are we seemingly incapable of imagining and experiencing much more compelling conceptions of diversity?

Behind our story of diversity is a larger story of the world, which comes with all kinds of assumptions, superstitions, and illusions. Any serious exploration of this story of diversity should attend to this much larger story. This is what rigor means. It means looking honestly and courageously at all the forces and influences that shape how we perceive and experience the world, and attending also to the implications and consequences. Though recognizing all of these forces and influences may most likely be impossible, what matters is whether our commitment to doing so is sincere. It is this sincerity that makes our moral evolution possible, thereby enlarging what we can believe, perceive, and imagine. Thus what should concern us most is why our popular story of diversity is so lacking in any kind of bold moral imagination.

This lack of imagination is the hallmark of academe. The techniques we use to produce knowledge are simply incapable of making any bold revelations. But the problem really begins with us. The way we continue to define and relate to knowledge impedes our capacity to engage the world with courage and fortitude. There is no challenge to deal with the world on its own terms, with all of its infinite ambiguity, mystery, and complexity. What emerges is an abstract knowledge, a knowledge that wants nothing to do with reality. What also emerges is a power devoid of any capacity to enlarge our sense of possibility. But, ultimately, what emerges is us and our ever-increasing anxieties, insecurities, and paranoia. This is the true consequence of how we continue to define and relate to knowledge. It dehumanizes us. It reduces us to objects of knowledge rather than creators of knowledge.

CHAPTER 9

ON THE NATURE OF IDEOLOGY

WRITING IS ABOUT CULTIVATING CONVERGENCE. It is about employing a certain technology to make our thoughts converge with words, and words to converge with other words to make sentences, and sentences to converge with other sentences to make paragraphs, and so on and so on. Writing is a struggle for coherence. But coherence is nothing but another of the many expressions of convergence. Coherence allows us to understand well the insidious nature of convergence. Behind this struggle for coherence is the belief that we have to struggle for coherence. This is why many contend that good writing requires hard work. It must be difficult and strenuous. We must write, rewrite, write, and rewrite. We must aspire to vanquish confusion, that is, divergence. We must discipline ourselves in order to discipline our writing. Supposedly, poor writing reflects a weak mind, one lacking in rigor and discipline. Coherence is a struggle—a struggle for order, for control, for clarity, for understanding, for civility, for prosperity. For what is the possibility for civility and prosperity without coherence, without convergence? Such is the insidious nature of convergence as ideology. Who dare argue against the need for convergence? Even entertaining the thought seems ridiculous, foolish, clownish. But such is the power of ideology. It shapes what is reasonable, plausible, and ultimately, possible. This is why opposing a dominant ideology is such a formidable undertaking. This is why those who try to do so often end up in mental asylums. There is no give. Nothing bends.

To argue against coherence makes believe that we are arguing for incoherence. Immediately the idea seems ridiculous, preposterous. To even begin to challenge the notion of coherence puts us in a perilous state. We have to begin to fight for our lives, our sanity. Nobody comes out of such a struggle in one piece. Something is always lost. There is always damage, always wounds. You are always in a fight for your life, and the prospects of prevailing are against you. The reason being that with any ideology the logic is self-ordering and self-reinforcing. To take on coherence requires us to take on the whole ideology, including all the institutions and structures that are creatures of the ideology. We must also take on the rationality, the sensibility, and the modality that come with the ideology, and actually function to protect the integrity of the ideology when threats arise.

Coherence is about our belief that the world is divided between opposing forces that are inherently in conflict with each other. Coherence is about us believing that life must be wrestled from death, just like how health should be wrestled from disease, order from chaos, communication from confusion, meaning from ambiguity, and so forth. Convergence is about conquering the world's supposedly malevolent forces, especially those that surround the flesh. The struggle for coherence is fundamentally about our determination to conquer the flesh, to impose order and limits on the flesh. This is why we associate coherence with reason and all that is good. It is about disciplining the body. This, again, is the problem with taking on the hegemony of convergence. We have to be ready to denounce all these beliefs, and the things these beliefs legitimize and encourage. This means being ready to be cast as strange.

Coherence is merely one expression of convergence. Assimilation and inclusion are also about convergence. So too are calls for compromise and unity. When we believe that a common language is necessary for stability in a linguistically plural society, that is convergence. When we believe that such a society should also share a common set of values, that is convergence. When we believe that schools should have a common curriculum, that is convergence. When we view diversity in terms of boxes, that is convergence. When we believe that certain issues are divisive and polarizing, that is convergence.

When we believe that market forces will make for a superior society, that is convergence. When we believe in speech codes and restricting speech, or believe that certain speech may be offensive, that is convergence. When we believe that we have a right to coercively impose our values on others, that is convergence. When we believe that hierarchy is both necessary and inevitable, that too is convergence. Moreover, when we believe that competition promotes prosperity, that is convergence.

So what is convergence? It is about believing that human beings have no inherent moral capacity or potentiality. Morality must therefore be imposed on us. Convergence is about what we do to realize a common morality. It is about eliminating and reducing anything that could even remotely undermine our achieving a common morality. Thus, with convergence, there is always a suspicion of diversity. There is always a fear, an anxiety that diversity could make for our undoing, and ultimately our demise. So regardless of how much we profess to value and celebrate diversity, we never leave it to its own devices. It is always in the presence of convergence and made in the image of convergence, which means that difference is always hassled, harassed, and policed. This is what happens when we believe that human beings have no moral capacity. We cannot be left to our own devices. We must always be controlled, assimilated, disciplined, monitored. All of this is convergence. Convergence is also all the fears, anxieties, insecurities, and paranoia that come with us believing that we have no moral potentiality. So what is convergence? Convergence is fear—fear of each other, fear of the world, fear of ourselves. It is about reifying these fears, legitimizing these fears, cultivating these fears, nurturing these fears.

Violence and convergence are inseparable. Convergence creates violence, encourages violence. But most of all, convergence normalizes violence. We will never achieve the coherence we desire because the world is simply too large for us to do as please. We will only achieve the illusion of coherence. Coherence is ideological rather than natural. It is a human invention. Yet we are still to believe that coherence is vital to how the world should be and needs to be. This, again, is how ideology works. It has this insidious way of shaping what we can imagine. But ideology is us. It is about what we are willing to imagine. There can be no ideology without us. Just as much as ideology makes us, we make ideology. Therefore to believe that we can simply rid ourselves of coherence by ridding ourselves of the underlying ideology is simply false. Coherence also comes from us. It appeals to something within us. Thus, even as I write now about coherence, I am still earnestly trying to achieve coherence. I am beholden to its fears. I cannot even fathom forsaking it. How will I begin to do so? I even wonder whether I will be ever ready to so. Of course I know well the ravages of coherence, or at least I believe I do. But then there are the social norms. What would become of me if I were to finally end this struggle for coherence? What would the end of coherence look like? In trying to achieve coherence you have to create divergence—that is, a foe, something that needs to be vanquished. For without a foe, there can be no struggle. The struggle for coherence is always a struggle against difference. It forces us to find something within ourselves that we despise, that we must come to believe is deserving of being vanquished. This is how the struggle begins and endures. Eventually, everything is normalized. We simply cannot imagine any other way of being. This is how we go about being in the world—by being in perpetual conflict with ourselves, by waging war upon ourselves and each other. We are always normalizing violence. Violence shapes everything about our being. For only through violence we can achieve coherence and convergence. If violence helps us make sense of ourselves, then surely violence can help us make sense of others. So violence becomes inevitable. It also becomes moral. But this is merely one way to explain the origins of violence.

There is the violence that is born of convergence. This is the mothership of violence. This is the violence that pervades everything, legitimizes everything, normalizes everything. This is the violence that is never even perceived or experienced as violence. This is the violence that is found in apathy and indifference, and also the violence found in vengeance and retribution, nihilism and narcissism, assimilation and inclusion. Without these ordinary kinds of violence, the violence found in war, slavery, and genocide would be impossible. Convergence makes for the origins of violence. The ideology of convergence would have us believe that this world, in being of dueling and conflicting forces, is born of violence. In order to at least survive, we must be able to subdue, manipulate, and even vanquish the forces that are inherently and supposedly hostile to us. Survival of the fittest means being able to distinguish the strong from the weak. It means being ready to exploit and even destroy the weak. It means being ready to separate our own fate from that of the weak. It means believing that our fates are separate. It means believing that all relations are shaped by deception, coercion, and manipulation. When convergence functions as ideology, we are to believe that our prosperity, even our survival, depends on us overcoming or at least lessening the divisions that supposedly divide us. This is why we believe in inclusion and assimilation. We must strive to achieve commonality, as in a common language, a common heritage, a common ambition. We are to believe that the story of Babel is about the perils of divergence. To avoid such a fate, convergence is supposedly necessary. By any means necessary, we must promote, cultivate, and impose commonality.

Once again violence becomes inevitable. Without violence, our demise will come to pass. Divergence will rule and difference will make for our undoing. In a world that believes in convergence, difference is always in peril. In fact, convergence creates difference. In a world of convergence, difference is other. It is that element that is always perceived as separate and outside of our being, that element that we believe is born of the malevolent side of the world, that element that we are morally obligated to vanquish. It is therefore that element that invokes within us the most fear, the most anxiety. Even though we continue to profess that we value difference, embrace difference, celebrate difference, in a world of convergence, where violence pervades everything, this valuing of difference is nothing but a farce. We create difference to legitimize violence. Without difference, there can be no violence, and without violence, convergence implodes. Violence sustains the ideology of convergence, just as much as convergence sustains violence. Difference is merely where all this violence plays out. Difference can therefore never escape violence in a world that values coherence and convergence. The most an ideology of convergence can do is either assimilate or tolerate difference. But any difference we can assimilate or tolerate really poses no threat to the status quo. In other words, neither process releases difference from violence.

So difference is a creature of convergence. This is why difference will never pose a threat to us. There will be no clash of civilizations. All of this commotion is merely what we need to believe, and of course, what we believe will shape what we perceive and experience. We need difference in order to legitimize our violence. Without difference, violence will have no ground. We therefore need to continually create difference. We need to make believe that difference is always at our throats. It is always threatening what is (supposedly) good, decent, and pure. Yes, pure. For what is purity? It is that which is pristine, that which is clean, sacred. In this case, what is difference? It is pollution, contamination, corruption. Yet without purity there can be no difference. However, as with everything else, there is no condition that is pure and pristine. This condition is of our own making. It is ideological. But we need to create this notion in order to legitimize our fear of difference, and ultimately, in order to justify the violence that difference must face. For how could we possibly do nothing to stop that which is pure and pristine from being contaminated, polluted, and corrupted? So by creating something that is pure and pristine, we also create difference. But we are also reinforcing the worldview that gives convergence credence by once again making believe that this is indeed a world divided between positive and negative forces. We are also solidifying the belief that this worldview is true. This is how the world really is. But most of all, we are also legitimizing all the fears, anxieties, and paranoia that circulate around difference. We are beginning the process of justifying all the violence that will soon come upon difference. Violence once again becomes inevitable. But this is a violence against us as there is nothing but us and what we need to believe.

Excellence is another insidious way we do convergence. We do so by refusing to acknowledge that epistemologies are really ideologies. We make believe that epistemologies are separate from ideologies. This separation allows us to believe that how we define, relate, validate, acquire, and experience knowledge has nothing to do with what we believe, value, or assume.

Once again we seek to divide and separate. Once again we want to find something to despise and eliminate. In this case, that something is mediocrity. Mediocrity will supposedly make for our demise. We therefore have to save ourselves from mediocrity. We have to cultivate and promote excellence. This means instituting all manner of rules, regulations, and protocols that will lead to excellence, and accordingly, make for the demise of mediocrity. Yet what we define as excellence is ideological. Of course the goal is to make believe that it is anything but. But it is all human. However, we wish to avoid this reality. Mediocrity is all about what we despise in the human experience, such as our susceptibility to all kinds of passions, impulses, and desires. This is why we associate excellence with rigor and reason. It supposedly constitutes the conquering of all the things that give rise to mediocrity. Thus besides reason and rigor, we also associate excellence with discipline and industry, such as our determination to abide by the rules, regulations, and protocols that will supposedly save us from mediocrity, and in so doing, save us from ourselves. This is always the recurring theme in convergence. Without elaborate structures to create and preserve order, we will supposedly descend into chaos and mediocrity. So in order to survive and flourish, we must aspire to remove or eliminate or erase or assimilate all the forces that lend for chaos and mediocrity, and be resolved in our determination to do so.

But what also emerges are those destructive dilemmas. As convergence is creating difference, it also is seeking to erase difference. Indeed, convergence is always demonizing difference so as to ready us for the violence that difference will soon meet. However, as convergence sets out to eliminate difference, it also creates difference. It cannot help but create difference because it needs difference. Without difference, convergence would be impossible. Convergence creates difference by trying to remove ambiguity. The goal of convergence is to drain the world of ambiguity. There can only be one meaning, one interpretation, one truth. But ambiguity is infinite. There can be no end to ambiguity, which means that there can never be merely "one" of anything. This is the origin of diversity. But difference is different from diversity.

Whereas diversity is ecological, difference is ideological. It is born of fear, anxiety, and paranoia. Race is difference. Ethnicity is difference. Sexuality is difference. Gender is difference. Difference, again, is a creature of convergence. It is about what we need something to be. But whereas difference is ideological, diversity is ecological. It constitutes possibility. Diversity resides in only those relationships that make for the rise of new ways of being that affirm life and possibility. In other words, whereas difference is life-negating, diversity is life-affirming. Difference is born of negation. To declare I am white is to declare I am not black, to declare I am heterosexual is to declare I am not homosexual, to declare I am male is to declare I am not female, and so forth. The purpose of difference is to separate and divide. But as we separate and divide we diminish our complexity, relationality, and ultimately, our humanity. We become more susceptible to convergence, and consequently, more and more susceptible to creating and reifying new kinds of difference. Through convergence we eliminate diversity by cultivating difference.

The goal of convergence is to help us avoid the world's infinite ambiguity, complexity, and diversity, and thereby make a world that conforms to our fears. However, human beings need the world's ambiguity, complexity, and mystery. These things challenge us to enlarge our ways of being, thereby enlarging what we are capable of perceiving, understanding, and ultimately, sharing. Such again is the divide between excellence and mediocrity. This excellence that we promote is no excellence. It too is fundamentally ideological rather than ecological. The goal of this difference is to impede the rise of diversity. In this case, this also encompasses the rise of other ideologies and epistemologies. In other words, the goal of this excellence is to impede the rise of new knowledges, including the theories, methodologies, and pedagogies that come with these knowledges. Yet all the while we profess to be committed to the creation of new knowledges. This is what excellence supposedly means. It means that we are rigidly abiding by the standards and procedures necessary for the formation of new knowledges, which also assumes that these are the standards and procedures necessary for the formation of new knowledge. This is how ideologies masquerade as epistemologies. This is how epistemologies do the bidding of ideologies. The knowledge we generate and celebrate as excellence will never pose a threat to the status quo. Such knowledge will only reinforce an ideology that makes us less and less vulnerable to other theories, methodologies, and pedagogies.

Then there is the matter of knowledge and experience. Who will dare call into question the notion that knowledge will set us free? It is supposedly ignorance that will keep us in bondage. So we are committed to achieving knowledge and vanquishing ignorance. Once again the ideology of convergence has us separating, dividing, and demonizing. Once again we are to believe that the world is divided between competing and dueling forces. Once again we must pick up arms and vanquish the supposedly malevolent forces that threaten our survival and prosperity. There is never any question which side we must take. Just as much as no fool would even dare take the side of mediocrity, no fool would take the side of ignorance. Such again is the power of ideology. But this is also what happens when we separate ideology from epistemology. The division between knowledge and ignorance is purely a human invention. What is also a human invention is how we define knowledge, relate to knowledge, experience knowledge, and purpose knowledge. To believe that knowledge will set us free from ignorance is all ideology. How did we come to believe that we were in bondage? How did we come to associate ignorance with bondage? This, again, is all ideology. We simply accept the association between ignorance and bondage, just as how we accept the association between knowledge and emancipation, as how the world really is. If, of course, this is how the world really is, then we need to cultivate convergence, which means finding the most effective ways—such as promoting excellence—to vanquish ignorance.

We are once again at war with ourselves. Once again we must believe that there is something wrong about us. We cannot be left to our own devices. Knowledge must be imposed on us through compulsory schooling and all the other compulsory things that come with compulsory schooling. Failure to do so will presumably make for the rise of ignorance, and all else that presumably comes with ignorance. Such again is the insidious nature of ideology. In addition to shaping how we perceive something, ideology also shapes how we experience something. But again, when we separate ideology from knowledge we make believe that knowledge is knowledge, and that we therefore share the same definition of knowledge. It is presumably any information we have derived from the world and that we have verified through elaborate processes. In short, knowledge is anything that is empirically verifiable. But this definition is all ideology, meaning this is how we need to define knowledge. After all, why should knowledge be empirically verifiable versus something else? How did this become the measure of knowledge, and why do we define knowledge this way when so much of the world will simply never lend for such verification? But this again is what happens when we separate ideology from epistemology. In doing so we mask the fact that everything begins and ends with what we believe and are willing to believe. Therefore in this case we need to believe that knowledge will save us, just as much as we need to believe that we have the ability to distinguish true knowledge from false knowledge. Yet history makes no case for knowledge. All of our greatest abominations (slavery, Jim Crow, the Holocaust) had nothing to do with a lack of knowledge. Nor does history point to any correlation between our moral evolution and our accumulation of knowledge.

But this is knowledge as we define knowledge. This is knowledge as something we can accumulate, manipulate, and exchange. This is knowledge as something that is inherently amoral. The morality supposedly resides in what we decide to do with this knowledge. This, again, is supposedly the knowledge that will set us free and save us from the ravages of ignorance. But what is the promise of this knowledge? Did this knowledge save us from the Holocaust or Jim Crow? Yet we continue to believe that this knowledge will set us free. This releases us from the courage and fortitude that are vital to engage all of the world's infinite ambiguity, mystery, and complexity. No doubt, life is difficult, often treacherous. It is also unrelenting. But most of all, life is ambiguous. There is simply no way to know anything for certain. This reality will always be unnerving and unsettling. It can also be frightening and crippling. On the other hand, this ambiguity can be invigorating, inspiring, and liberating. But this stance to ambiguity requires courage and fortitude, which we can only achieve by doing things that are hard and difficult. However, we have taken the path to limit ambiguity, to resist ambiguity, to vanquish ambiguity. Thus the emergence of convergence as ideology. In every expression, the goal of this ideology is to vanquish ambiguity. We believe we can simply do so by eliminating the malevolent forces that supposedly promise to ruin everything. For instance, the ideology of convergence would have us believe that confusion is the antithesis of communication. Achieving communication presumably means conquering confusion. By cultivating convergence, either by using a common language, or trying to achieve common meanings for different things, we supposedly achieve communication. However, the vanquishing of confusion is theoretically impossible, comparable to trying to drain the oceans of water.

There is no need to vanquish confusion. In fact, confusion is integral to the human experience. It vitalizes what we are capable of sharing and understanding. Without confusion, communication would be impossible. Yet we persist in trying to vanquish confusion. By any means necessary we aspire to achieve convergence. This is the violence that is inherent in how we define and experience communication. But such again is the persistent nature of convergence. There is always violence, and the violence always begins and ends with us. We are always the site of violence. We eventually become immune to the violence and begin to have no qualms about even the necessity of violence. With convergence comes the most insidious relationship with violence. Violence becomes ordinary. It is what we supposedly do, and need to do. Indeed, without violence, there can be no convergence. Therefore if there is to be any possibility of us achieving a world devoid of violence, we have to find the courage and fortitude to rise above the ideology of convergence. We have to be willing to enter into a different relationship with the world's ambiguity.

The ideology of convergence victimizes all of us. As much as we believe in and strive to promote convergence, eventually convergence turns on us. But we never notice the violence, or how we participate in the violence. So we never notice that all the great prophets were victimized by this ideology of convergence. But we continue to strive for convergence, and as we do the violence becomes more pervasive, and we become more and more cruel. So note the violence that comes with indifference. There is no violence that is more dehumanizing and disfiguring. There is also no violence that is more insidious. As much as slavery, Jim Crow, and the Holocaust were extraordinary acts of violence, such violence would have been impossible without the violence of indifference. It is therefore easy to believe, as we now tend to believe, that the worst is behind us. Due to the rise of convergence we have supposedly morally evolved to recognize that these great acts of violence were moral abominations. But what to make of the violence that is now threatening to end the planet, or the violence that is making for the proliferation of weapons of mass destruction, or the violence that is making for the unparalleled incarceration of so many human beings for non-violent offenses, or the violence that is widening the gap between the world's rich and poor? These acts of violence are no less abominable, and no less reflect our indifference.

Violence produces indifference, just as much as indifference produces violence. The ordinary acts of violence that convergence promotes impede the making of empathy and compassion. Such acts of violence cut us off from each other. This is how we become amenable to believing in survival of the fittest and other such theories that celebrate a self that seeks its own self-interest. This is also how we come to believe in the inevitability of hierarchy. Convergence pushes us to find ways to rationalize our indifference as well as our violence. On the other hand, indifference makes us susceptible to theories that rationalize our indifference. So everything becomes self-fulfilling. We believe what we are capable of believing. Yet this does nothing to change the fact that our indifference cuts every which way. Our indifference to others is also about our indifference to ourselves. Our indifference to ourselves is also about our indifference to the planet. The violence of indifference cuts every which way because our lives are intertwined. This is probably the oldest moral teaching. It is at the heart of all the world's great scriptures.

Every prophet said something about us being our brother's keeper. This reality is also most evident in the natural world. But the ideology of convergence would have us believe otherwise, and we continue to be willing to believe otherwise, as coming to terms with this truth would change everything. It obligates us to do things that require extraordinary courage, as in the courage to love, to empathize, to forgive. Convergence saves us from such courage.

This is what makes convergence so seductive. Courage is about being ready and willing to die. There is nothing natural about courage. We have instincts and impulses that guard against doing anything that threatens us. Courage is about doing something that is inherently unnatural. This is why courage is moral rather than natural. Courage allows us to rise above the pull of our primal instincts and impulses that seek to keep us safe and secure. Nothing is fundamentally wrong about us possessing these natural instincts and impulses. But this is merely one dimension of our humanity. We also have moral, relational, ecological, and spiritual dimensions. We need the flourishing of all these dimensions in order to live well. This is why courage is important. Only through courage we can love and do all the other extraordinary things that make us human. Without courage, we are nothing but cowards. We have no capacity to empathize, to forgive, to love, and most of all, no capacity to act with passion, conviction, and imagination. We act as cowards do, laden with all manner of fear, anxiety, and paranoia. Motivation must come from outside of us, either in the form of threat or reward. But of course as soon either disappears, action stops. We become paralyzed, crippled. Desperation emerges.

Eventually alienation is all but certain to happen. This is the condition that convergence thrives on. It impedes our capacity to act with passion, conviction, and imagination by crippling us with all manner of fear, anxiety, and paranoia. However, by constantly trying to remove the world's ambiguity, complexity, and mystery, convergence impedes the evolution of courage. It reduces us to cowards, and for cowards, only convergence makes sense. Cowards lack, besides empathy and compassion, any kind of rich moral imagination. For cowards, only coercion and retribution are plausible courses of action. This is also what makes the coward a threat to all of humanity. Devoid of any moral imagination, the coward is hostile and fearful of anything and any person that he perceives as a threat to his worldview. He lacks the courage to be vulnerable. Deception, deceit, and duplicity are the hallmarks of the coward. Yet there is a price that comes with such ways of being. The coward is always susceptible to alienation. He is tortured by all manner of desires, motives, instincts, fears, and impulses. The lack of vulnerability makes the coward a closed system, which makes for all kinds of neuroses and psychoses. This is how the coward comes to have a twisted and distorted view of the world. He perceives and experiences the world through these neuroses and psychoses. The world is always conspiring against the coward. His existence is always in peril. Because of all the neuroses and psychoses, the coward is incapable of dealing with the world on its own terms. He desires safety and security in a world that will never guarantee neither. In this way, the coward is always in conflict with the world, always bent on doing something to the world to have security and safety. But only futility arises, which only further exacerbates the coward's many neuroses and psychoses. So the coward is always in a state of anguish, desperation, and confusion. He is trying to have a relationship with the world that is simply impossible, yet everything he does to attain this relationship only further pushes him into the abyss of alienation and despair.

All that is certain to come from this dire situation is increasing violence. But this is where the ideology of convergence enters into the picture. It offers the coward a way to make sense of the dire situation, even to find some sense of hope. It also gives the coward a way to make sense of the violence and to tolerate the violence. However, no amount of convergence can change the fact that our violence, regardless of however legitimized, falls back on us. The fallout is always ugly. Indeed, what is most evident about the ideology of convergence are the many illusions, such as our believing that we can continue to exact the amount of violence we do on the planet and still make it out alive. As much as we profess to have an unsurpassed knowledge of the world and the human experience, we continue to hold to these kinds of illusions. Nothing could be stranger. For what more knowledge do we need in order to understand that this ideology of convergence will eventually make for our undoing? But then again the problem was never a problem of knowledge. This too is another of those illusions that comes with the ideology of convergence.

Every ideology is a story of how the world is and needs to be. The purpose of hegemony is to hide this reality. We are to assume that our view of the world is really how the world is and should be. Therefore the purpose of hegemony is to impede the rise of other narratives, especially conflicting narratives. But of course hegemony is us. It reflects our unwillingness to engage or even tolerate other narratives. This hostility to diversity is by no means news. It is instead developmental, or moral. We have to acquire through exercise and practice the capacity to engage and cultivate other narratives. This involves the ability to recognize that our own narrative is fallible. It is a human invention, made from the resources that are available to us. In being a human invention it comes with all manner of illusions and superstitions. Yet nothing is inherently wrong or limiting about this reality. It merely serves to remind us that we are fallible, and therefore everything we create will be no less so. That we are fallible means that we should be humble. We should treat nothing we create as infallible, as something we cannot change, revise, or even forsake. This is how we create false gods. But this is what hegemony conspires to do. It seeks to make us believe that we are infallible, and thereby believe that all we create and value is no less so. However, when such is the case, how could we possibly be willing to explore and engage other narratives? What would be the purpose of doing so? The project of hegemony is to deny our fallibility. This is why hegemony can only afford one truth, one understanding, one meaning.

To deny our fallibility is to deny everything that makes us human. It is, in fact, to deny the best of everything that makes us human. Without our embracing our fallibility, vulnerability is impossible. That is, embracing our fallibility makes empathy and compassion possible. Fallibility means we make mistakes, even when our intentions are noble. In this way, fallibility promotes mercy and forgiveness. In recognizing our own fallibility we recognize the fallibility of others. Embracing our own fallibility therefore encourages us to be generous in our judgment of others. In short, fallibility promotes grace. All these things—mercy, forgiveness, grace—make us human. We can no doubt criticize hegemony for blocking the rise of new narratives. But this criticism still misses the damage hegemony inflicts. Hegemony diminishes our humanity. It makes us less human. This is why every major prophet warned us about worshipping false gods. No tendency is more destructive. The world seems determined in every which way to make plain to us that we are inherently fallible. Everything we value and assume to be true begins with something we believe. There is simply no way to divorce this relationship. All we have is the illusion of doing so. But this again is what makes the worshipping of false gods such a destructive practice. Eventually, illusions produce all kinds of fear and paranoia. This is how hegemony rises, by seeking to rationalize all these fears and paranoia. But this is also why hegemony is ultimately destructive.

Hegemony undermines our ability to perceive the world through empathy and compassion. This is why hegemony usually comes with violence. But note the power of our illusions. We even pretend to own the notion of rationality. Yet there is nothing rational about us. For what is rational about our destruction of the planet, or the proliferation of weapons of mass destruction? Infallibility cultivates hypocrisy. We pretend to be the most open-minded, when in fact we seem to be the most close-minded. We also pretend to be the most just when reality paints a different picture. But this is what narratives do. In our story of the world there is hypocrisy. This again is what hegemony allows us to do—to suppress anything that threatens the integrity of our narrative. It saves us from the struggle that comes with being fallible. But this is a struggle we need. Because we are fallible we have contradictions, confusions, tribulations, and frustrations. To be fallible is to recognize that we will never conquer the world's infinite ambiguity. What is unknown will always exceed what is known. Embracing our fallibility humanizes us. It blesses us with doubt. Doubt pushes us to look again and again at everything we believe and value. Doubt reminds us of our fallibility. We will never be gods, and as a result, have no business acting like ones. Indeed, doubt challenges us to question everything. This is the beauty of being fallible. Because we are fallible we can appreciate the fact that the world is laden with possibility. There is always the possibility for a new meaning, a new understanding, a new truth, a new reality. Without doubt there can be no possibility, and with no possibility there can be no diversity. Diversity is the affirmation of possibility. So through doubt we remain open to possibility. In other words, only through doubt are we capable of believing in the possibility of God.

Fallibility means that no human being would ever profess to have a perfect understanding of God. It reminds us that there is no need to have such a conception. For why would we want to limit what God can be—that is, to make God in only our image and likeness? What would this do for us? How could fallible human beings ever possess the power to have a complete and absolute conception of God? Our fallibility reminds us that such a conception will never be ours, and that to continue to seek such a conception will only make for peril and despair. Through our fallibility God is great because God now becomes boundless. By embracing our fallibility we bring possibility into the world. Yet we persist in our destructive ways, and with our persistence comes nothing but violence. The violence is always inevitable as we are trying to do something that is simply contrary to the order of the world. We are trying to limit the world's diversity. However, when we aspire to impede possibility, we put the world in peril. For what seems all but certain is that this is a changing and evolving world. It moves towards the creation and cultivation of possibility. This is why no fallible being would ever aspire to have a complete conception of God. Such a conception of God would limit possibility, as in the possibility of other conceptions of God, other relations to God, and even other obligations to God. In short, such a conception would diminish God, and in doing so, also diminish us. But again, why would we want to impede the possibility of a conception of God that is beyond our own imagination? What good or purpose would doing so serve?

Possibility means that there is always the possibility for a conception of something that is superior to our own. But instead of being about enlarging what is possible, we are about determining what is true. There is hardly much that is constructive in trying to determine what is true. Such a project assumes that the world is divided between truths and falsehoods. What we determine to be true is also what we profess to value and believe. Yet what we determine to be true begins and ends with what we value and believe. In other words, before we can determine something to be true, we must be ready and willing to believe that it can be true. Consequently, there are only certain truths we deem to be valuable. Thus as much as we like to believe that we are beholden to determining what is true, nothing could be further from the truth. It is all a pretense to save us from coming to terms with our own fallibility. This is why the enterprise of science continues to seduce us. But there are always implications and consequences that come with our actions and lack thereof. To promote illusions is to live by illusions. A much more constructive enterprise would have us focus on enlarging what is possible. This enterprise assumes that this is a world of infinite possibility, and what matters in the end is whether we are creating conditions and promoting practices that nurture possibility.

The travesty of convergence resides in its determination to end possibility by trying to limit the world's infinite ambiguity. To converge is to assimilate. However, that which cannot be assimilated must delegitimized, marginalized, persecuted, and sometimes even eliminated. There can be no alternatives with this ideology. It is either assimilation or persecution. This is why prophets always face persecution. For in the face of convergence, what can a prophet do? But of course every prophet constitutes possibility. This is why prophets matter. Prophets seek to enlarge our sense of what is possible. This is why prophets always pose a threat to the status quo. As much as the world is waiting for the coming of the next great prophet, our continuing hostility to possibility means that all that is certain is that this person will face our wrath for threatening the order of things. There is simply nothing else we can do within an ideology that is hostile to possibility. Violence is always inevitable. So there will be no coming of a next great prophet, or at least any we are capable of recognizing and appreciating. But the loss, as always, will purely be ours. Until we can evolve away from the ideology of convergence, our redemption will continue to elude us. We will remain mired in misery and mayhem. Our increasing indifference will bring only death and destruction, and our hypocrisy will continue to be without end. The coming of another prophet to save us is purely of our own making. It serves to release us of responsibility for all the violence that we continue to bring into the world. Ultimately, we aspire to escape our own complicity in all the consequences that flow from our actions and lack thereof.

To disown responsibility keeps us separate and outside of each other. It allows us to believe that our fates are separate. There is supposedly no inherent responsibility to care for the well-being of others, such as concerning ourselves with all of our actions and lack thereof. However, we diminish our humanity by denying such responsibility. Being human means choosing various courses of action and owning the responsibility that comes with all the consequences and implications that flow from our actions and decisions. Action is the foundation of everything. There can be nothing without actions. But the fact that all our actions have implications and consequences means that the responsibility for such actions falls on us. We must own all the implications and consequences, which means recognizing that our actions always affect others. This recognition enlarges our humanity. It pushes us to recognize that our fates are intertwined. It also pushes us to recognize that our humanity is bound up with the natural world. Owning responsibility for our actions and lack thereof changes our ways of perceiving the world. It also expands our moral imagination by pushing us to look thoroughly at all the possible implications and consequences that flow from our actions. Moreover, as no action emerges from a vacuum, owning this responsibility also encourages us to look at all the forces that are shaping our actions and lack thereof. Thus in every way the cultivation of responsibility humanizes us by pushing us beyond our limits. Of course many would contend that we already promote responsibility. We presumably do so by promoting market forces that reward responsible actions and punish those that are less so. In fact, this is the case that is principally made for the institution of market forces—the promotion of responsible behavior. This is supposedly how markets promote civility and prosperity.

But in reality markets undercut responsibility by promoting competition, which in turn promotes distrust and suspicion. By promoting self-interest, as in survival of the fittest, markets limit responsibility to purely that which serves our own self-interest. Responsibility is supposedly about doing what is necessary to safeguard our self-interest. We assume that this kind of responsibility will make for all kinds of reciprocity, which in turn will make for the foundation of a robust society that requires barely any government regulation. But this will never be the case as a responsibility born out of self-interest can hardly be defined as responsibility. This constitutes a distorted notion of responsibility. The problem begins with the view of life that forms the foundation of this ideology. It assumes that life is about the promotion of self-interest. Through the promotion of self-interest we mate, reproduce, evolve, and survive. This ideology assumes that our lives are purely of our own making and that our fates are separate. But we are ecologically, psychologically, and communicationally intertwined. Self-interest is a human invention. It is ideology. We are ecologically, psychologically, and communicationally obligated to be responsible for the well-being of others. This responsibility is inescapable. It is built into the natural order of the world. We can merely pretend to have no binding obligation to others and the planet. But the pretension comes with the promise of much peril. So as many advocate for the unleashing of market forces, what is most apparent is the rampant lack of responsibility that simultaneously emerges. It was always our unwillingness to own our responsibility for the well-being of others that made for all the world's great horrors.

But the worst is still yet to come. There can be no possibility of an enduring and flourishing democratic and pluralistic society without a rich conception of responsibility. The increasing loss of responsibility means that we will have to increasingly rely on coercive and punitive devices to achieve any semblance of order. We will be forced to continually develop more elaborate devices as our notion of responsibility disintegrates. But eventually no amount of devices will suffice, and our full savagery will be unleashed on the world. There must no doubt be consequences that come with our persecution of so many prophets. Of course it would be nice to believe that soon a God will intervene and save us from our worst selves. But why? Why should any God want to intervene? What promises to be different after such an intervention? What could we possibly promise to do differently that we are not fully capable of doing now? Certainly, the problem was never knowledge. We always knew that vengeance and violence were abominations, and that love, mercy, and compassion have a lot to do with our redemption. But why us? Why should any God want to intervene only for us? What about all the other species that abound upon the planet? What about us is more deserving of an intervention when we have, by our own doing, made for so much death and destruction?

But this is what happens when we reduce God to our image and likeness. Our own narcissism becomes unbound. In fact, with any ideology of convergence, narcissism is inevitable. Convergence is about the imposition of our truths, our beliefs, and our values on others. Convergence assumes that our truth is the only truth. This is why narcissism is inevitable. In order for convergence to thrive we must believe that our truth is the only truth. There must be no doubts, as doubts encourage dissent, and dissent makes for rebellion. Of course we always profess to be welcoming of dissent as we are presumably a democratic and pluralistic society. But convergence makes both impossible. In fact, there is nothing democratic and pluralistic in what we define as democratic and pluralistic. We define democracy in terms of representation. But we can always have representation and still have no resources or power to accomplish anything. This is the plight of minority representation. In our definition of democracy, only the representation of the majority matters, and the majority only requires the narrowest margins in order to rule. When majority status is achieved, the representation of the minority becomes all but null and void. Either way, representation has no creative or generative capacity. A majority is under no obligation to engage other positions, especially those that come with the least representation. There is therefore nothing to stop the majority from becoming corrupt.

A much more heuristic way to define democracy is in terms of possibility—democracy is about being committed to the promotion of practices and environs that create and generate possibility. Here democracy assumes a world of infinite possibility. There is always the possibility for a more heuristic way of doing something, understanding something, conceptualizing something. In a democracy nothing is off limits, which is to say that there is no regard for orthodoxy. Orthodoxy impedes possibility by insisting that the past is reliable. There is therefore no need for disruption and the attending risks that come with doing anything new. Risk means uncertainty. It also means exploration and discovery. But most of all, risk means courage, as in the courage to explore the impossible. Through democracy we also explore the nature of the obscene and profane. What we commonly define as such is usually merely another way of foreclosing on possibility—that is, another way of avoiding the courage to explore the impossible. This is the problem with viewing democracy in terms of representation. It undermines courage. Why, again, should the majority be willing to take any risk that could jeopardize its status? Also, why should any group be willing to take more risk than is necessary to achieve majority status? In short, representation undermines our ability to act boldly and courageously. It promotes fear, such as the majority always being afraid of anything that could jeopardize its status and power. In the case of representation, courage is death.

Nothing good comes from the absence of courage. As much as we would like to believe that our model of democracy reflects our moral superiority, history would beg to differ. Slavery, Jim Crow, and the Holocaust were all creatures of our common conception of democracy, so also the proliferation of weapons of mass destruction and our destruction of the planet. The persecution of every prophet also has origins in our common conception of democracy, as when Pontius Pilot asked the people to vote on who should be pardoned. There is simply no case to be made that the decision of the majority is morally superior to that of any minority. Thus why should any model of democracy favor the actions and decisions of the majority?

Many claim that majority rule is simply more humane than being subject to the tyranny of any minority. Such may no doubt be the case. But what about the tyranny of the majority? Tyranny, regardless of whether practiced by the majority or minority, is still tyranny. But this is supposedly the reason for different branches of government. However, such checks and balances did nothing to save us from slavery or Jim Crow. In fact, all these branches sought to do the opposite. Only through protests and extraordinary sacrifice did these abominations expire. That is, only through courage did justice come forth. It was courage that put an end to the tyranny of the majority.

CHAPTER 10

ON RIGHTS AND OBLIGATIONS

Do HUMAN BEINGS HAVE *RIGHTS* or *obligations*? Moreover, in a world where our fates are intertwined, and one that faces increasing peril, either from proliferation of weapons of mass destruction or ecological implosion, what is best for us to have, *rights* or *obligations*? The United States Constitution claims that we have rights. Yet African Americans had to wait over 350 years before achieving these rights. Still, every pursuit of liberty begins on the premise that we have rights. We accuse government of making laws that infringe our rights. We profess the right to marry who we wish, to have access to birth control, to live where we want, to have an abortion, and to carry weapons.

We treat liberty and rights as inseparable. Liberty is about the right to do as we please, as long as we never impede upon the rights of others to do likewise. It also involves stopping government from violating our "inalienable" rights. Rights assume individualism. Supposedly, our lives are outside and separate from each other. Thus how I exercise my rights has no bearing on others, meaning that others have no right to infringe upon my rights. Who I choose to love and marry has no bearing on who others choose to love and marry. So rights are about live and let live. We each determine our own ethics and morality. Rights also supposedly mean the right to defend our borders. It also means the right to go to war to protect our interest and way of life. But again, what is the value of rights in a world that is increasingly making plain to us that our fates are intertwined and that our own humanity is shaped by the humanity of others?

Our minds are shaped by relational and metaphorical forces. No mind is born of isolation and separation. Our actions and decisions always have consequences for each other. Still, is the notion of rights constructive? Does it help us live peacefully and democratically? Can it help us deal productively with the tensions and gyrations that come with our unfolding world? Such a case is difficult to make. Reality seems to have finally caught up with the notion of rights.

Individualism is an illusion. It means that I am a product of my own making, captain of my own destiny. Individualism means that I am only responsible for my own actions and decisions. I have no obligations to others. I am merely to mind my own business and live my own life. However, individualism only works in a world where we are unwilling to believe that mind is relational and metaphorical. But because mind is relational and metaphorical, relationships are the foundation of everything. We have obligations to each other, such as an obligation to create relationships that are rich in all manner of resources. We are also obligated to treat others tenderly and compassionately as our treatment of others falls back on us. That the condition of our humanity is also bound up with the condition of the world also means that we have obligations to the natural world. We have to treat the natural world with care and reverence as our treatment of the natural world also falls back on us. What becomes of the natural world will determine what becomes of us. The notion of rights assumes that the natural world has no inalienable rights. Only human beings apparently have inalienable rights. We have, as a result, no qualms about trashing, abusing, exploiting, and despoiling the natural world. Only human beings apparently have rights.

The notion of rights is primal. Rights mean survival of the fittest. It means that my survival and prosperity is purely my own responsibility. Therefore I have the right to do anything to safeguard my survival and prosperity. My own well-being is first and foremost. The invoking of rights is always heard loudest when concerns arise about safety and security, especially our own safety and security. Yet human beings are by no means only primal beings. We are also relational, existential, spiritual, and ecological beings. We are embedded within a world that requires the cultivation of different kinds of relationships. Our prosperity, even survival, is dependent on our ability to build and sustain all kinds of relationships that are rich in trust, empathy, affirmation, and generosity. Without such relationships and resources, being human is all but impossible. We would be left to only our primal instincts and impulses, resulting in a world that is laden in distrust, suspicion, and paranoia, such as one that is obsessed with guns and the right to own guns. In such a world, safety means arming ourselves to the hilt. It means viewing others suspiciously. We must be ready for every contingency. Our right to own a gun is about our right to always carry a gun, even in schools and churches. Threats are apparently everywhere.

But this is how the notion of rights distorts our reality. Being embedded within relationships that are rich in resources fundamentally alters our view of the world by releasing us of the fear, anxiety, and paranoia that result from isolation. We perceive a much less hostile and threatening world. We recognize our humanity in each other by our ability to be vulnerable to each other. The notion of rights makes no sense in a world where human beings are assumed to be inherently relational in nature and being. It is a creature of a certain kind of world and perpetuates that world. However, besides making for a certain kind of world, the notion of rights also makes for certain way of experiencing the world that heightens our primal instincts and impulses. Again, rights are always about my rights, such as my right to control my body, my right to free speech, my right to own a gun, my right to protect my property and resources, my right to consume and purchase what I desire, and so forth. There are no rights that deal with helping others, or caring for others.

The notion of rights is about self, meaning that personhood is reduced to selfhood. I am presumably a human being because I possess a self. To violate this self is to violate my personhood. What emerges from this focus on making the self inviolable is egotism and narcissism. Ideally and legislatively, the goal is to have the least amount of constraints on the self, and the most strenuous case has to be made to add any new constraints. In theory, the self should be unbound as much as possible. We should supposedly have the right to protect ourselves and control our destiny. We should also be saved from customs and traditions that insidiously encroach upon our rights. Presumably, the world should have no right to impose any constraints on us. What constraints exist should purely be of our own making. In other words, the notion of rights assumes that the world is inherently devoid of any moral calculus or any moral constraints, or that it comes with no moral obligations. The limits of rights end with my simply having no right to deny you the rights I enjoy. We have, in theory at least, the right to do everything else, and any attempt to limit our rights must be brought before the courts for scrutiny. However, all of this assumes that personhood begins with selfhood. We supposedly each have a self that is the locus of all actions and decisions. In this case, the self should be inviolable. But again, this notion of self is an illusion. Personhood is relational rather than individual. Our relational resources shape and influence what we become. We are also ecological beings. Personhood is bound up with the condition of the natural world.

Our ecological resources also shape and influence what becomes of personhood. This, again, is why our relationship to the planet comes with obligations. No relationship is amoral. Relationships can evolve or devolve, meaning that relationships enrich us or diminish us. Just as well, relationships can enlarge what we are capable of experiencing and understanding, or undermine what we are capable of experiencing and understanding. Relationships are bound by certain parameters that lend for different outcomes and consequences. These outcomes and consequences bear directly on our lives and what ultimately becomes of our worlds. Thus instead of asking what is just, we should really ask what is relationally and ecologically best for all of us. Which actions and decisions are most relationally and ecologically enriching? Or, which actions and decisions enlarge what is relationally and ecologically possible? To recognize that we are ecological beings is to recognize that these actions and decisions represent our obligations to the world and each other.

CHAPTER 11

ON WHITENESS STUDIES

THE NOTION OF COMMUNICATION BEING epistemic is extremely profound. It assumes that the world is laden with infinite possibility, and that we are bound up with the world. What we do shapes and influences what the world becomes and in turn what becomes of us. We make our worlds by how we choose to experience the world and ourselves. We are therefore in no way at the mercy of a world that is separate and outside of us. Neither are we of a world that is unalterable and unresponsive. That the world is responsive and communicative means that the onus is on us to be responsive and communicative in our ways of being. It also means that the onus is on us to cultivate the most responsive and communicative ways of being, so we can allow the world to be responsive and communicative to us. Together, both mean that communication is a human-making, world-making practice. Communication is the womb of possibility.

What is really at stake is recognizing and understanding what is possible. Of course we are to believe that truth is what matters. The truth will supposedly set us free, meaning that the truth will release us from ignorance. This is the epistemology of truth. In this epistemology, communication is a tool to express our thoughts. It is merely the symbolic and linguistic means we use to share our truths. But there is nothing redeeming about this epistemology. This epistemology assumes that truths reside in a world that is outside and separate from us. We create methodologies and technologies to find these truths, and theories to make sense of the truths we believe we have found. But all of this is nothing but an illusion. This supposed world that is outside and separate from us is a creation of our own imagination, or really the lack of. We created this world, including all the fixtures and furnishings. This world is merely a reflection of what we imagine ourselves to be, or what we imagine to be possible. It reflects a certain way of relating and communicating to the world, even a certain way of embodying and experiencing language. Ultimately, this world reflects a certain way of being in the world. What we imagine the world to be is bound up with what we imagine ourselves to be. We can demonstrate this by merely looking at how we arrive at our supposed truths. Our methodologies already assume a certain vision of the world. That is, our methodologies already know what is in this world, or what is to be found and what can be found. The process of discovering truths is really about uncovering truths. We are only capable of understanding what we are capable of imagining.

But what of gravity? Indeed, what of gravity? Gravity also belongs to a certain vision of the world. It is something that is perceived, languaged, and narrativized, just as much as the sun is perceived, languaged, and narrativized. To say that gravity is real is different to saying that gravity has meaning. Many things are real, such as all the pebbles on beaches being of different sizes, but yet these things have no meaning to us. To give something a meaning is to give something a value, a purpose. Our narratives determine what value and purpose we attach to different things. But because we conceive our worlds, our methodologies will find everything these worlds assume to be valuable. We will then announce how we are progressively unmasking the world and revealing its mysteries. We will credit our methodologies and technologies for affording such progress. We will then demand submission to these truths. The worlds we conceive eventually begin to conceive us. We become our own fictions.

This is why there is nothing heuristic about this enterprise of discovering truths. Truths are our own inventions, born from a conception of the world that is lacking in imagination. So yes, gravity is a truth. But what gravity means, and what value we associate with gravity, is a different matter. Perception, observation, and imagination are all bound up with each other, meaning that there is no separation between mind, body, and spirit.

Meaning requires a story, a narrative. What gravity means involves locating gravity within a certain story of the world. Our own narratives shape what things mean. But our narratives begin in what we are ready to imagine, to believe, and experience, and in turn eventually come to shape what we imagine, believe, and experience. Every narrative presents a different set of possibilities, meaning that narratives are morally unequal. Narratives that lend for the most possibilities are the most heuristic or the most productive. An epistemology of possibility is committed to the exploration of possibility, including removing practices that impede possibility, and promoting those that promote possibility.

Human diversity is just like gravity. It is real. It also belongs to a story of how we imagine the world to be. Our story of diversity stresses themes of inclusion. Inclusion is a good thing in our story of diversity. We value inclusion and assimilation. We also understand diversity in terms of differences, but only certain kinds of differences. Many kinds of differences have no meaning for us, and are thus excluded from our story of diversity. But diversity can never be included, welcomed, or accommodated. Inclusion means assimilation. In order for diversity to be included, diversity must become something other than diversity. Plurality, possibly. But the most insidious threat to diversity comes from those who profess to be committed to the inclusion of diversity and even view themselves as representing diversity, meaning those who view diversity in terms of race, gender, ethnicity, sexual orientation, and disability, and especially those who are increasingly involved in the promotion of Whiteness Studies with the aim of exposing and ending white privilege. To begin with, who is against exposing and ending white privilege?

But what exactly is white privilege? Generally, Whiteness Studies defines white privilege in terms of racial norms. It is about being advantaged simply because of being of such norms. Whiteness Studies focuses on exposing these white racial norms. No doubt, white racial norms are privileged and do shape what behaviors are acceptable. But defining whiteness in terms of race is like defining an ocean in terms of water. Yes, an ocean is a body of water, but viewing an ocean in terms of water misses the fact that an ocean is also a vast ecology that is responsible for creating and sustaining an extraordinary amount of life forms. Whiteness is no different. It is a worldview. It speaks to certain way of imagining, perceiving, engaging, and being in the world. Besides a racial component, whiteness also has ideological, epistemological, and institutional components. As with any hegemony, whiteness has the institutional means to coercively and even violently erase, displace, and marginalize other worldviews.

We know exactly what whiteness is. We know what it believes, what it values, how it behaves, how it perceives the world, and how it makes sense of the world. We also know well its ability to destroy. No other worldview is responsible for much death and destruction. No other worldview has also put the world in so much peril. Yet Whiteness Studies continues to treat whiteness as a racial norm and in terms of racial subjectivity. If we can only come to terms with our own white privilege, apparently all will be well. Whiteness Studies claims to be about the politicizing of whiteness. Instead it depoliticizes whiteness by reducing whiteness to a racial phenomenon. There is no reckoning with the worldview, and by that the ontology and epistemology, that brings whiteness into the world.

Whiteness Studies poses no threat to the status quo. It fetishizes white privilege. White privilege becomes nothing but a racial thing. In fact, Whiteness Studies is an invention of whiteness and white privilege. We are to assume that our problems are fundamentally racial in origin. Fix our race problem, and apparently all will be well. We are to assume that exposing white privilege is integral to doing so. But viewing our problems in terms of race, though by no means an invention of whiteness, is an obsession of whiteness.

Whiteness Studies deepens this obsession by further reifying the belief that race matters, especially when that race is white. Indeed, race matters, and being white comes with all kinds of privilege. But why does race matter? How did the invention of race and our obsession with race come about? What forces brought this destructive thing into the world? For nothing good has come from this invention. To borrow Ruth Frankenberg's words, race is "arguably the most violent fiction in human history." Yet, as seen in the rise of Whiteness Studies, our obsession continues. In many ways Whiteness Studies averts our attention from the worldview that is responsible for this obsession.

No worldview can ever give rise to the means for a new worldview. This is why Whiteness Studies is the most that can be had in our current worldview and exposing white privilege poses no threat to the status quo. White racial norms are increasingly disappearing into ideological and political norms that will probably soon end our obsession with race. Thus, Whiteness Studies increasingly warns about mistaking the end of race for the end of white privilege. We are to be vigilant and on the lookout for racism without racists. Again, for Whiteness Studies, racism is apparently the evil that torments the world, just as how Women's Studies assumes that sexism is what torments the world. But would ridding the world of racism, sexism, heterosexism, and so forth save the world from the creation and proliferation of weapons of mass destruction, or our own destruction of the planet?

We should all desire a world devoid of white privilege. But why should such a world be the limit of our imagination? What about the possibility of a world without war, poverty, hunger, and all manner of human misery? Where is the case that exposing and ending white privilege gets us to that world? That world involves the building of a new worldview, with all new ideological and epistemological components. Whiteness Studies, like Women's Studies, and other such studies, besides offering no resources that can help with such work, also distracts from the doing of such work. We remain obsessed with race, and in so doing bound to a worldview that is obsessed with race. We therefore continue to perceive and make sense of the world through race (or gender, or sexual orientation). If race matters, then racial privilege matters. What also matter are the racial norms that come with whiteness. But again, race is an invention. Race, too, is like gravity. Yes, our colors and shades are different. But what those differences mean begins with us. What meanings we give to these shades and colors depend on our story of the world. This story shapes how we perceive and make sense of the world, which in turn validates what we imagine the world to be. Because of psychological forces and pressures, such as the need for cognitive coherence, we are always striving to make our story coherent. We are inclined to believe things that are in harmony with what we already believe. Our imagination matters. This is the problem with Whiteness Studies. In keeping us obsessed with race,

Whiteness Studies keeps us bound to a worldview that is of an impoverished imagination.

All ways of imagining are by no means morally equal. Every imagination reflects a different moral vision. In order to achieve a world devoid of war, destruction, and misery, we need a new imagination. We need to find ways to induce new imaginations. Rather than merely imagining ourselves as racial beings, what about imagining ourselves as relational beings, or communal beings, or ecological beings? These represent much more heuristic and expansive ways of imagining the human experience, and also make for new narratives that can help make for a world with much less cruelty and misery. This is the indictment of Whiteness Studies. It keeps us trapped within an impoverished imagination that gives us no way of dealing with issues and struggles that exceed race. White privilege is no doubt a blight on the world. But there was cruelty and misery before white privilege, and most certainly there will be cruelty and misery after white privilege. White privilege is by no means our original sin. Our original sin deals with our failure to imagine the world and ourselves in really extraordinary ways, which again begins with our being ready to believe in extraordinary things. Especially for those of us who are black and brown and have to put up with the ravages of white privilege, viewing the world racially is seductive. It requires hardly any imagination. This seduction draws us to Whiteness Studies. We know best the corrosive and destructive nature of white privilege. We dream of worlds devoid of white privilege. But such is also the insidious nature of Whiteness Studies. Who is influencing what kinds of worlds we dream of? Why should such worlds only be devoid of white privilege? What about dreaming of worlds that are also devoid of all the other horrors like war, hunger, and ecological destruction? How can we begin to dream of such worlds? As long as we continue to believe and perceive things in terms of race, we will continue to dream in race. Even if those dreams are devoid of white privilege, the presence of race makes nightmares inevitable. New worldviews come from new imaginations. That we are already capable of imagining the human experience in new ways (relationally, communally, ecologically) reminds us that our imagination remains boundless.

CHAPTER 12
ON DEFINING THEORY

TO ASK THE PURPOSE OF communication is also ask the origin of communication. What is communication *for* and *why*? The popular view is that communication is a linguistic and symbolic process that allows us to share our thoughts and emotions with others for purposes of achieving superior forms of organization and coordination. This view claims that what distinguishes us from other species is our evolved linguistic and symbolic capacity, which in turn is responsible for our superior levels of coordination and organization, and which in turn is responsible for our superior civilization. So the purpose of communication is to facilitate our evolution, meaning that communication is born out of evolutionary necessity. There is supposedly nothing moral or spiritual or ecological about our purpose. Neither does communication supposedly have any moral, spiritual, or ecological foundation. It is merely a tool, and consequently, only requires mastery.

This is the story that the western/European world has long been peddling and successfully propagating. We are fundamentally biological beings, products of evolution. In this story of communication human beings are "survival machines." Our primary purpose is to procreate and propagate our genes. Moreover, according to this story, procreation requires deception and manipulation. We are constantly scheming, always seeking to put ourselves in the best evolutionary position. We have always been seduced by a primal and biological conception of the human experience. Such conceptions make no moral demands on us. We can freely indulge our primal instincts and impulses. This is how the world becomes laden with war and other kinds of horrors. Such actions become tolerable and justifiable. This is supposedly how the world is. The strong will prey on the weak. This is also how the world should be. We should allow the strong to prey on the weak. How else, apparently, would the weak become evolutionarily efficient? Or, how else would the weak become strong and achieve better prospects of surviving and prospering? In this story what is good is whatever serves the cause of our survival and prosperity. If creating and stockpiling weapons of mass destruction stops or dissuades others from invading our lands, or taking our resources, or threatening our interests, thereby threatening our own evolutionary interests and prospects, then such actions are good (moral). What is moral becomes simply a matter of determining what serves our own evolutionary interest.

But what of altruism? It is the problem that even biologists acknowledge refuses to go away. There is nothing about altruism (sacrificing our own lives for strangers) that serves our evolutionary interests. So is altruism less moral than stockpiling of weapons of mass destruction? What also to make of the social relationships between members of different species (which biologists now refer to as unlikely friends) that have nothing to do with symbiosis or reciprocity? Neither do these relationships have any origin in the different species sharing a common symbolic and linguistic system. Thus how exactly are these different species forming these relationships that reflect enormous trust and affection?

We become what we imagine ourselves to be. We also define things by what we imagine ourselves to be. Indeed, everything begins with what we imagine ourselves to be. Of course, many would contend that our theories are descriptions of things. Others contend that our theories are interpretations of things. But I would contend that our theories are imaginations of things. Theories reflect what we imagine things to be, which begins in what we imagine ourselves to be. I therefore have no interest in assessing the accuracy of our descriptions of things. Neither do I have any interest in determining the power of any theory. Instead, I am interested in the imagination that makes for the creation of a certain theory, as well as the imagination that is seduced by such a theory. Every theory asks to believe something, imagine something. Before we theorize, we imagine. Success becomes inevitable, as our theories will always accurately describe the world we imagine. After all, what else can our theories describe? So in many ways, quarrelling over the accuracy of any theory is pointless. What should concern us is whether the theory enlarges and challenges what we imagine ourselves to be. What new vistas and possibilities become available to us? Yet on the other hand, every theory is born out of a certain imagination. Theory development should be about inducing new kinds of imaginations. It must be much more than a conceptual exercise, such as trying to determine how accurately a theory describes the world. It should also be an emotional exercise, an existential exercise, a spiritual exercise, and yes, even a communicational exercise. We can continue to argue about a theory's validity. But again, in many ways every theory is valid. We can also continue to argue about whether the world needs theory—that is, about the usefulness of theory in creating change. We can also continue to argue about the proper relationship between theory and praxis. But all of these discussions assume a certain definition of theory. A theory is a tool, a device, a framework, an apparatus that allows us explain and understand. But again, this definition of theory misses the fact any theory is merely describing what we are imagining. We would be better served by defining theory in terms of being. To theorize is to imagine. In other words, to theorize is to induce new ways of being that enlarge what is possible. A theory is something we become. It speaks to a way of being rather than merely a device for explaining. As such, how do we begin to cultivate and promote more productive ways of being?

To treat theory as a device that helps us describe the world is to treat theory as something that is outside and separate from us. Theory also becomes this thing that deepens our belief that the world is outside and separate from us. In these ways theory becomes dangerous by being complicit in creating and reifying various illusions. There is no world from which we are outside and separate. We are always in the world, always experiencing the world, interpreting the world, perceiving the world. What should concern us is what are we construing the world to be? What is involved in construing the world in ever more expansive and imaginative ways? Indeed, the real illusion is believing that theory development has nothing to do with the heart, the spirit, the body. We approach theory development clinically and abstractly, the same way a craftsman approaches the making of a new tool. We focus on testing the theory, determining the theory's rigor, and figuring out the scope of the theory. Like a good tool, a good theory should be durable and dependable. As such, a lot of theory development is about showcasing a theory's validity by applying it to different settings and populations. We use theory to describe what we believe is going on out there in the world that is outside and separate from us.

We remain oblivious to the fact that what we are describing is merely what we are imagining. This is how our doing of theory becomes complicit in protecting the status quo. It removes us from the equation. It keeps the focus on what is being described rather than what is being imagined. It would have us believe that theory is performing this invaluable function. It helps us describe the world, and in so doing, presumably helps create a knowledge that is reliable and dependable. Theory is supposedly helping us build a superior knowledge, which in turn is presumably vital to the creation of a superior civilization. So whereas other civilizations have stories, ours have theories. That our knowledge is built around theory is supposedly what makes our knowledge superior, and ultimately our society superior. In contrast to stories, theories can supposedly be proven and disproven. Yet our own understanding of theory is nothing but a story. When we imagine we narrativize—we give a story to the world. The idea of theory is merely a character in our story. Yet there is nothing as compelling as storying. That the world's mystery is boundless means that the world lends for an infinite amount of stories. It also means that every story is fallible. There will never be a story that explains everything. That the world's mystery is boundless also means that every story is laden with fictions, things we need to believe for the sake of narrative coherence. It also means that we need to exercise epistemological humility. In the end, we are all storying.

We would be better served by approaching theorizing as storying. It would help us view theorizing as a creative and imaginative process. We would come to understand that theory development is about moral development, relational development, spiritual development. It encompasses all of our being, challenges all of our being. Theory development transforms our being. It also makes us better human beings by reminding us of our own epistemological limits. For again, no theory can end the world's mystery. Theory is as much a conceptual as a moral undertaking. To look at the world anew begins with us being existentially and spiritually ready to do so.

CHAPTER 13

ON DIVERSITY AND IDENTITY

EPISTEMOLOGICALLY, IDEOLOGICALLY, SPIRITUALLY, AND MORALLY, I never found identity—in terms of race, ethnicity, gender, sexuality, and so forth—to be a constructive construct. I have always struggled with which box to check. That is, which box can I fit into, or which box can contain *all* of my humanity, or which box can even begin to capture all of the ambiguity, complexity, and mystery that come with my own human experience? Practically, I understand the need to pick a box. Resources, though often minimal, are usually at stake. So I still choose the box in that context that is the most disenfranchised, and thereby could benefit the most from my choice.

But I remain tortured by the process, and now I want the torment to end. It has nothing to do with my parents being of different races, or even my grandparents being of different corners of the world. It is about Audre Lorde and why liberation can only begin with the rise of new tools. Can identity build the house of the slave, and thereby be both a tool of the master and the slave? How could identity serve two fundamentally different causes, that of oppression and that of liberation? No doubt, the master has always needed identity. For what would be the possibility of slavery, apartheid, Jim Crow, the Holocaust, and other such abominations without identity? But what did identity ever do for the slave? Why should the slave be bound by a conception of identity (this box business) that requires us to diminish all of our diversity, complexity, and ultimately, our humanity? So after checking "Black", what to do about also being a father, a husband, a brother, a teacher, an uncle, a vegetarian, a pacifist, an animal rights activist, an immigrant, a mentor, an anarchist, and of a spiritual tradition that draws from all of the world's great religious teachings? How could all these other things have nothing to do with being Black? According to Cornel West, race matters, meaning identity matters. But matters for whom, and for what purpose? Yes, in regards to inclusion, identity matters. But when did the politics of inclusion become emancipatory, or the politics that best serves the cause of diversity? This, after all, is the same politics that created affirmative action to devalue, displace, and delegitimize reparations. This is also the same politics that would have us believe that diversity needs inclusion rather than revolution. So again, can the tools that build the house of the master also build the house of the slave?

Any rigorous and robust approach to framing and promoting diversity needs to acknowledge four key premises: (a) various peoples have been historically marginalized and disenfranchised, and the legacy of such discrimination and exclusion remains enduring; (b) dominant and prevailing institutional practices do reflect and favor the ideological and material interests of various peoples, and thereby are inherently hostile to peoples of different interests; (c) as much as viewing diversity in terms of race, ethnicity, gender, sexuality, and disability is important, such a multicultural approach also masks and suppresses other kinds of diversity that are no less important, such as ideological diversity, epistemological diversity, pedagogical diversity, historical diversity, spiritual diversity, and existential diversity—that is, diversity in terms of being and knowing; (d) finally, all supposed expressions of diversity, and even claims of diversity, are by no means morally equal, meaning that only those ways of being and knowing that expand our limits of possibility genuinely qualify as diversity. Taking these premises seriously means looking diligently and critically at how our institutional norms and practices undercut diversity, and consequently, the entry and flourishing of perspectives that can be enriching and life-affirming.

But all of this constitutes a different way of defining the struggle for diversity. Indeed, what happens when your own struggle for diversity is different, and even conflicts with the common struggle for diversity? That is, what happens when you insist on viewing diversity in ways that exceed race, gender, sexual orientation, and disability, and thereby have no regard for any struggle for diversity that focuses on the inclusion and accommodation of differences? What also becomes of your own struggle for diversity when the status quo prefers to do business with the popular struggle for diversity, and is even able to use this struggle to undermine your own struggle? No doubt, after 350 years of slavery, Jim Crow, and Jim Crow Jr., race matters, and will long matter. Various peoples have been historically marginalized, disenfranchised, and brutalized. These truths are beyond dispute. But how did inclusion become the best way to ending our harming of each other?

We seem to be assuming that various peoples were merely historically excluded for being different. If such were the case, then inclusion is arguably a just solution. But African Americans, especially, were by no means merely excluded for being of a different race and ethnicity. For over 350 years, African Americans were enslaved, tortured, and brutalized. How could inclusion be a just solution for all of this misery? What also of our obligation to vanquish the epistemological practices that made for all this misery—that is, ending the tools that made for the building of the master's house? In my view, any rigorous struggle for diversity must reckon with understanding the origins of this misery and dismantling the epistemology that made for this misery. Viewing such misery racially uncomplicates our understanding of this misery. For even viewing persons in terms of race is an epistemological matter. But viewing diversity in terms of epistemology would make for a different struggle for diversity. It would mean looking at diversity in terms of being and knowing. It would also mean looking at diversity in terms of emancipation rather than inclusion.

There are many falsehoods at the core of our common understanding of the struggle for diversity that make impossible any redemption of this enterprise. There is, again, the falsehood of identity, that our supposed identity (diversity) can be put neatly into boxes. In reality, any attempt to box our identity only diminishes our diversity, and ultimately, our humanity. There is the falsehood of equality, that inclusion promotes equality. If so, what to make of the widening gap between rich and poor in this age of diversity and multiculturalism? There is also the falsehood of diversity, that diversity is about our differences. If so, what to make of our unwillingness to value, include, and celebrate those differences that culturally and religiously oppose our *chosen* differences? Then there is the falsehood of tolerance, as in the need to be civil to each other. This is civility functioning as a rhetorical apparatus to subjugate, discipline, and assimilate diversity. To invoke civility in the name of tolerance is to privilege our sensibility. We are insidiously demanding that others share and even comply with our own sensibility. But the sharing of a common sensibility is homogeneity rather than diversity. If anything, diversity must at least mean that what I view as civil can be fundamentally different to what others view as civil. Thus why should I be rebuked and disciplined for refusing to comply and conform to your notion of civility? How did your definition of civility become so privileged as to possess the ability to discipline other kinds of civility?

Further, there is the falsehood of inclusion, that inclusion and assimilation are good. We are to assume that diversity can be included and accommodated, and this is a good thing. So diversity discourses are always highlighting the supposed virtues of diversity and how promoting diversity makes for good business practice. Diversity is always encouraged to apply. However, the inclusion of diversity also means the assimilation of diversity. Diversity must conform to the norms, customs, and expectations of the status quo, meaning that inclusion involves accepting and even acknowledging the dominant paradigm as superior. The burden is on diversity to adapt to the status quo, meaning that the onus is on diversity to conform and submit.

Inclusion conspires to keep epistemology on the margins. To perpetuate a certain kind of writing is also to perpetuate a certain way of understanding the world, relating to the world, embodying the world. In this case, to believe that scholarly writing should be about "specificity and precision" is to also believe that the world lends for "specificity and precision" and that we are capable of deriving both from the world. But many native and indigenous peoples throughout the world would claim that the world in no way lends for such "specificity and precision" and that it is our foolish pursuit of such "specificity and precision" that is responsible for all the harm and peril that is now upon the planet. Indeed, inclusion means limiting our attention to conceptual and methodological issues, such as bringing the experiences of minority peoples to dominant theories and methodologies. However, no theory or methodology comes out of a civilizational vacuum, or a historical and epistemological vacuum. In fact, no theory of knowledge comes out of a civilizational vacuum. Failing to look critically at the civilizational context from which our theories and methodologies are born impedes the struggle for diversity. We are encouraged to miss the fact that the enterprise of producing new kinds of theories and methodologies is different to that of merely producing more theories and methodologies, and that new kinds of theories and methodologies can only come from the rise of new epistemologies.

Finally, there is the falsehood of mutuality, that we can achieve diversity without disruption or even revolution. This falsehood is responsible for the prominent role of dialogue and dialogic circles in the common struggle for diversity. But to view diversity from the perspective of epistemology is to realize that disruption and revolution are necessary for the coming of diversity. Epistemologies are like tectonic plates, always grinding and colliding against each other. Seismic and cataclysmic disruptions are inevitable, but also necessary for life's prosperity. The planet would be devoid of its boundless diversity without the violence that comes from these moving tectonic plates. In an increasingly plural and multicultural world, collisions between different peoples, just like tectonic plates, are inevitable and necessary. Tension and conflict must happen as hegemony is always at stake. We all want our worldview to rule the world. We want others to share our beliefs, our truths, our values, such as our valuing of diversity. We want others to share our value of homosexuality and gender equality. We want others to deny the diversity that comes with honor killings, genital mutilation, and other such cultural practices that conflict with our own morality.

There are consequences that come with all of these falsehoods that pervade the common struggle for diversity. We continue to define diversity in terms of race, gender, sexual orientation, and disability, thereby helping to suppress the diversity found in our different rationalities, sensibilities, spiritualities, and modalities, as well as the diversity found in our different histories, ontologies, epistemologies, and axiologies. Our common diversity struggle is bereft of any means of navigating all of this diversity and complexity. Yet in helping the status quo strip us of all of this diversity and complexity, our common diversity struggle also helps the status quo degrade our humanity. We are reduced to merely objects of inclusion that promise certain material rewards, like helping our employers gain entry into new minority markets. Lost in the common struggle for diversity is the fact that our supposed exclusion was fundamentally an epistemological matter. How did we come to perceive others in ways that would encourage us to enslave and brutalize those persons? How did this come to make sense to us? How did we intellectually legitimize all of this misery and brutality?

There is also the consequence that comes with believing that diversity can be included, thereby reducing the struggle for diversity to simply removing those obstacles that block the entry and flourishing of diversity. What emerges is an obsession with identifying those persons and practices that either overtly or insidiously do so. The goal is to create a safe and nurturing space for diversity, one where diversity is valued and embraced. But diversity can only be included by being assimilated. That is, the common diversity struggle perpetuates the illusion that diversity can be included, and that diversity should strive to be included. But inclusion degrades diversity, depoliticizes diversity, emasculates diversity. Inclusion strips diversity of diversity. In aiding and abetting the status quo in every which way, the common struggle for diversity becomes fully complicit in degrading diversity. In order for diversity to be diversity, neither inclusion nor assimilation can be viable options. Diversity must embrace exile and all the tribulations that come with being marginalized and disenfranchised, harassed and forsaken. It must be ready to never enjoy the resources and privileges that come with being included and assimilated, such as Bayard Ruskin and Audre Lorde never being fully embraced by even the Black community. It must also be ready to never have the safety and security that come with inclusion and assimilation. Diversity must be ready to find the most creative and innovative ways to make do. But even on the margins, the status quo will demand that diversity enjoy no peace. There will always be incursions into the supposed badlands. So there will always be skirmishes. Diversity requires resolve and fortitude. We must be ready to endure and struggle.

Diversity is much more than merely different ways of perceiving the world. It is fundamentally about different ways of imagining and reimagining what the world can be. Any rigorous struggle for diversity should be about liberating and emancipating our imagination. Indeed, this is ultimately my problem with the common struggle for diversity. It degrades our conception of identity. We continue to view identity in terms of who we are and which box we belong to. But again, to view identity this way erases our diversity and complexity. It diminishes our humanity. How we construe identity also reflects a lack of moral and epistemological imagination, an unwillingness to look at the world anew. This leaves intact a status quo that continues to brutalize diversity by promoting conquest. It also makes people who have been historically marginalized and brutalized complicit in the oppression of diversity, such as civil rights leaders publicly condemning Martin Luther King, Jr. for opposing the Vietnam War. The struggle for diversity becomes nothing but the oppression of diversity. A new conception of diversity implicates a new conception of identity. In my case, I define identity in terms of possibility because I define diversity as the affirmation of possibility. I view identity as a conceptual space, a space of possibility. It is a space where I imagine and explore new ways of being in the world. I am committed to the nurturing of this space, and also to furnishing this space with all the relational and epistemological resources I could possibly need. It is the cultivation and protection of this space and these kinds of spaces that I view as the struggle for diversity.

CHAPTER 14

On Being and Knowing

KNOWLEDGE IS PRESUMABLY A GOOD thing. It means progress. Thus being committed to acquiring more and more knowledge is presumably a good thing. It is something we should value and promote. Being knowledgeable means possessing something that is valuable. Being knowledgeable therefore makes us valuable. We determine our value by what we know and how much we are capable of knowing. What kind of knowledge we possess and where we acquired our knowledge define our worth and status. Consequently, credentials matter. Credentials allow us to distinguish who knows what and how much. That is, credentials allow us to distinguish who, in being more knowledgeable, is more valuable. Credentials therefore allow us to categorize each other. That credentials matter means that institutions matter. Institutions award credentials, as well as protect the integrity of the credentialing process. Institutions therefore play a vital role in determining and comparing our worth. We are valuable only when and after a credentialing institution declares us to be so.

But how did we come to equate knowledge with human worth? How did being knowledgeable become so valued? Did slavery result from a lack of knowledge? Did Jim Crow? Did apartheid? Did the Holocaust? In short, what horror can we blame on a lack of knowledge? Why then is knowledge so valued?

Our worlds are products of our imagination. What is true in our worlds begins with how we perceive our worlds. What we therefore define and value as knowledge begins with what we imagine and perceive the world to be. In fact, even the idea of knowledge and what being knowledgeable means begins with what we imagine and perceive the world to be. As much as we treat our idea of knowledge as something natural and eternal, all ideas are of our own making. But how constructive and productive an idea is a different matter. History vividly reveals that all ideas are by no means morally and ecologically equal. Our idea of knowledge begins with us being at the center of the world. To know means that we have the power to know, are entitled to know, and that the world is knowable. Such an ethos permeates our knowledge.

We produce knowledge for the sake of conquering the world. Knowledge presumably allows us to manipulate world. The more knowledge we have, the more power we presumably command. This is how we evaluate different cultures and civilizations. Which cultures and civilizations have the most knowledge? We believe that the supposed superiority of various civilizations comes from the fact that such civilizations simply have the most knowledge. This is how we situate our own civilization. We are presumably the most advanced civilization the world has ever seen because we have the most knowledge the world has ever seen. We have also made the greatest investment in generating and propagating knowledge. Our supposed success is also validated by the fact that other civilizations are rushing to adopt our view of knowledge and model our institutions of higher learning. However, with our vast knowledge generation and knowledge propagation apparatuses, we are still responsible for the most devastation and destruction the world has ever seen. If our vast knowledge is responsible for our success and superiority, then how best to explain all of the death and destruction that was the hallmark of the western/European world in the last century? How would our success have been possible without our ravaging of the planet for natural resources? How did our vast knowledge do nothing to stop World Wars I and II, and all the other unsurpassed horrors? In short, how could our vast knowledge be only responsible for our success?

But many will contend that our knowledge is neither responsible nor culpable for our successes and failures. Our knowledge merely gives us the means to do different things. We decide how to use knowledge and to what ends. We are ultimately responsible. But this view lacks coherence. On one hand, we are to attribute our civilizational success to our knowledge. We claim that our knowledge makes us morally superior by removing us from our primal instincts and impulses. The pursuit of knowledge supposedly civilizes us. The process instills rigor, rationality, and objectivity. It subdues our emotions and passions, biases and prejudices. We become cultured, civilized, and sophisticated. We develop certain habits of mind and being that can apparently only come from the pursuit of knowledge. These habits of mind and being are presumably what make for our civilizational success and superiority. Our civilization is superior because we are superior. This is why only our civilization can apparently be trusted to have weapons of mass destruction. We alone apparently have the temperament and restraint to use these weapons responsibly. This is also why we apparently have a moral obligation to police the world and be the world's moral beacon. Our unrelenting pursuit of knowledge has supposedly made us morally superior. But again, if we are morally superior, what explains our unsurpassed devastation and destruction of the planet, as well as all the death and misery that marked the last century?

There is a lot about this enterprise of knowledge that is seductive. The idea of us possessing the ability to reveal the world's deepest secrets is appealing. The idea of us being able to do things that no other species can do is no less so. However, in a world of boundless ambiguity and mystery, what and how much can we really profess to know? What kind of reliable and dependable knowledge can we achieve in such a world? But how else can we explain our success and superiority? We are apparently achieving a knowledge that is allowing us to conquer the world. We will therefore continue to believe that knowledge is possible. We can gain dominion over the world, and thereby control our fates. As a result of our knowledge we can manipulate the world in ways that favor us. Presumably, without being able to gain dominion over the world, we will, like every other species, be at the mercy of the world, vulnerable and defenseless. Viruses will kill us, hurricanes will drown us, storms will swallow us, and so forth. This is why and how knowledge gives us power. The more of the world's secrets we can unlock, the more power we gain over the world. The more knowledge we amass, the more powerful we become. We therefore have a stake in believing that we are capable of conquering the world's boundless ambiguity and mystery. We need to believe that we are indeed making important "breakthroughs" and "unlocking" the world's "deepest secrets." Such supposed successes matter deeply to us in terms of shoring up our beliefs.

But all we are unraveling and unlocking is merely what we are imagining and perceiving the world to be. We are also only answering the questions we are capable of asking, framing, and answering, thus the supposed unbending and unyielding march of science. We view science as merely doing its own bidding. Presumably, science is beholden only to science. We are merely the beneficiaries of its successes and accomplishment. This is why we are advised to never interfere or get in the way of science. To do so is to disrupt our own progress. But the march of science is nothing but our march. The ambition of science is nothing but our ambition. Consequently, the illusions of science are nothing but our illusions. How we perceive the world shapes how we make sense of the world, and what means we use to do so. Our worlds will always make sense to us. Our theories and methodologies will collude to make sure that such is always the case. In our case, there is simply too much at stake for anything else to happen. We need to believe that we are capable of unraveling and unlocking the world's deepest secrets and mysteries. For what will become of us if we are unable to do so? How will we justify our supposed superiority?

But the world has apparently begun to push back. This is a world of limits, and the world can bear only so many illusions. Eventually, a world of boundless ambiguity and mystery will remind us what boundless ambiguity and mystery really mean. We will never achieve a knowledge that will allow us to command this ambiguity and mystery. No doubt, many would contend that the ambition rather than the destination is what matters. We should avoid tossing out the baby with the bathwater. We should uphold the ambition of trying to acquire and accumulate as much knowledge as possible. But we are still beginning with the belief that trying to unravel the world is a good thing. That is, we still believing that our redemption resides in our pursuit of knowledge, even a certain kind of knowledge. The perils and horrors that are now upon us obligate us to challenge this belief. Why is this the only path to our redemption? Where is the proof that this path is best for us? What other cultures and civilizations are responsible for as much death and destruction? Which others have made as much peril and horror? In sum, is the world facing a crisis of knowledge or really a crisis of being?

We continue to assume that there is no relation between knowing and being. This is why we have theory and praxis, education and vocation, book sense and common sense, theorists and activists. Such divides are of our own making, so that we can continue to believe that knowing has no relation to being. However, our own evidence shows that the more knowledge we acquire, the more narrow-minded we become. Such evidence is threatening the story we have long been telling ourselves about the many virtues of being knowledgeable. But there is now a much larger concern that needs our attention. How did we separate being from knowing? Where did this separation occur? In reality, the separation never really occurred. It was always illusory. Our beliefs shape everything, influence everything. Being begins with what we believe and what we are willing to believe. To theorize is to believe. There is no knowing without believing. If there is a problem with knowing, the problem originates at the level of being. So if our ways of knowing are failing to challenge us, then the problem resides at the level of being. Something we believe is impeding us. In this case what is impeding us is the belief that we can reveal the world's deepest secrets and mysteries. This belief promotes neither humility nor vulnerability. Instead, this belief fosters a spirit of conquest. To know is to command, to control, to move from vulnerability to certainty. For us, knowing is about moving from weakness to strength. Therefore any challenge to what we know, or profess to know, is really a much larger threat. It is a threat to our strength, our security, our power. We will experience any such threat as a negative thing. There will be fear and anxiety. We will naturally try to find ways to delegitimize and neutralize such threats. Either way, we are disinclined to engage such threats openly and honestly. To do so requires vulnerability, and our goal is to move from vulnerability to certainty. For us, vulnerability means weakness, as well as discord, doubt, and confusion. We value and desire a being that is full of certainty rather than vulnerability. This is why we privilege homogeneity over diversity, commonality over plurality, stability over chaos. Being vulnerable is ideologically unnatural to us. But this unnaturalness is of our own making.

In a world of boundless ambiguity and mystery, our being anything but vulnerable is destructive. Vulnerability makes for a different relation to the world, and implicates a different kind of being. Vulnerability means that the world is rich in possibility. There is always the possibility for a different meaning, a different understanding, a different solution, a different process. Vulnerability embraces possibility. It also embraces the diversity that possibility invites, as well as the fluidity and complexity. Vulnerability is about being at peace with the world's rhythms and tensions. We are released of any anxiety that incites us to impose any one meaning, or understanding, or reality on the world. Vulnerability means humility, including ideological humility, epistemological humility, and spiritual humility. Vulnerability recognizes that any one interpretation of God diminishes both God and us by limiting what God can possibly be, and what we can potentially become.

Our civilization continues to suffer from a crisis of being, a crisis of vulnerability. Nothing is fundamentally wrong with trying to unlock and unravel the world's secrets and mysteries. But are we vulnerable in doing so? We are vulnerable in terms of recognizing how our beliefs are shaping what we are perceiving, experiencing, and understanding; vulnerable in terms of recognizing where our beliefs are emerging from; vulnerable in terms of recognizing why we are seduced by certain beliefs and subconsciously hostile to others. Vulnerability is about minding all the forces that shape our being, as well as the consequences of those forces and experiences. Besides shaping how we perceive things, what we believe also shapes what we value and how we organize our worlds. To be oblivious to what we believe is to be oblivious to our involvement in creating our worlds, and the responsibility that comes with such a role. To be oblivious in this way makes us reckless and promiscuous. This is how the project of knowledge seduces us. It masks our involvement in creating our destructive worlds. It allows us to assume that the world is outside and separate from us. Supposedly, our only task is to figure out how the world works, which means, of course, acquiring as much knowledge of the world as possible. Such an enterprise supposedly has nothing to do with us, or with what we believe, assume, and value. We are merely to choose a theory and methodology and begin hacking away at the world until we shake something loose. In fact, the enterprise insists that in every way we remove ourselves from the process so that our observations can be pure and free from our own subjectivity. This is the beginning of the removal of being from knowing. It also represents the beginning of our own separation from ourselves. Our separation from the world begins in our separation from ourselves. This is also where our recklessness and promiscuity begins, the recklessness and promiscuity that is responsible for all the devastation and destruction, misery and peril.

Vulnerability is about recognizing ourselves in each other, and recognizing ourselves in the world. Through vulnerability we recognize that we become what becomes of our worlds. This is why being accountable and responsible for our actions matter. However, by continuing to separate knowing from being, the world will remain in peril. On the other hand, to be released of any responsibility for the condition of the world and each other is deeply seductive. It places no demanding moral obligation on us. We can do as we please, or merely what serves our own self-interest. This is how ideology and epistemology are bound up with each other. To be separated from the world is to have no responsibility for the world. This is why the status quo values science. Science protects the status quo, legitimizes the status quo. As long as science assumes that the world is outside and separate from us, nothing can ever come from science that threatens the status quo. Science is now doing what religion long did. We are to assume that science is merely describing our world, revealing immutable truths. Our own interest would presumably be best served by submitting to these truths. We do differently at our own peril. That these truths from science generally serve our own self-interest and release us of any responsibility for the condition of the world just happens apparently to be a plus. But in this case these supposed truths are a minus. These truths are merely our truths. Science is about us wanting truths that have nothing to do with us. Truths are descriptions of this world that we assume is outside and separate from us. This is what Darwin's theory of evolution constitutes. He is describing a world that is outside and separate from us, and of course professing to do so objectively. He apparently has no role in this separation. He is merely objectively describing how the world really is. There is no recognition that every theory is really giving us an interpretation rather than a description. Every theory asks us to believe something, and succeeds by being in harmony with what we believe and imagine the world to be. Any theory that comes from science requires us to believe that the world is outside and separate from us. However, this belief, as even quantum theory is beginning to demonstrate, is an illusion. But rather than focusing on how this belief is illusory, what should concern us is the measure of this belief's productivity. In posing no threat to the status quo, what is the value of any theory that can do nothing to end our destructiveness? In fact, what is the value of any enterprise that actually encourages our own destructive impulses?

Ending the false divide between knowing and being will change much. The doing of inquiry will be different. Our theories and methodologies will be different. Even our questions will be different. Ending the divide between knowing and being involves ending the divide between mind and body. Now we must find the origins of our questions within ourselves. What beliefs are creating and legitimizing our questions? How do our questions bear upon the world? In the end, collapsing the divide between knowing and being will change the purpose of inquiry. No longer will the purpose of inquiry be to accurately describe a world that we assume is outside and separate from us. Instead, inquiry will be about describing our limits. What forces and experiences impede us from imagining the world in new ways? What beliefs constrain how we frame and perceive things? What structures and institutions impede the rise of new ways of being and becoming? We will attend to being as we attend to knowing. There can be no expansion of knowing without any expansion of being. We expand our being by deepening our capacity to be vulnerable to things that are even outside of our own imagination. Our limits are found in our vulnerability. How vulnerable we are capable of becoming will determine what we come to know and learn and understand. Thus inquiry should attend to our own vulnerability. It should expose and challenge what we are willing and unwilling to be vulnerable to. There are all kinds of ideological, institutional, and communicational forces that impede our vulnerability. Nothing should be outside our purview. But enlarging our vulnerability needs to involve much more than probing and dismantling the practices and structures that shape what we are willing to be vulnerable to. It must also involve cultivating those practices that deepen our vulnerability, and in so doing deepen what we are capable of knowing, learning, and understanding. Moreover, to expand what we are capable of being and knowing is to expand what worlds we are capable of perceiving and imagining. Attending to being is by no means merely an ideological and epistemological exercise. It is also an existential and spiritual exercise. Because the worlds we are describing are of our making, how much we come to know, learn, and understand will depend on how extraordinarily we can imagine and perceive these worlds. Imagination matters. How much we are capable of imagining will depend on how vulnerable we are capable of becoming.

Every theory belongs to a story of the world. We have always assumed that life is a struggle. We survive and prosper by beating back the forces of nature. This involves figuring out how the world works and using this knowledge to manipulate the world to our advantage. The more knowledge we are capable of generating, the more power we achieve over the world, ultimately enhancing our ability to survive and prosper. We continue to believe in this narrative. In this story, knowledge is a tool. We treat knowledge as an indispensable tool. Without knowledge, nature will end us. Our survival and prosperity depends on us having as much knowledge as possible. Knowledge also becomes a precious commodity. Because knowledge gives us power, we believe that the value of knowledge can be quantified and measured. Our survival and prosperity also depends on us developing more and more powerful technologies that will allow us to reveal everything. Such is the story and trajectory of our knowledge enterprise. Besides revealing what we believe, a narrative also reveals how we imagine ourselves to be and what we imagine the world to be. Changing the purpose of inquiry and our relationship to knowledge involves changing our story of ourselves and the world. This, in many ways, is what every prophet sought to do. That no prophet is yet to succeed should remind us of the hold that our narratives can have on us. In shaping what we believe and imagine, our narratives shape what we know and understand. Even the best narratives tend to be self-fulfilling and self-perpetuating. This is why we struggle immensely with change. This is also why we tend to be hostile to prophets.

We continue to contend that the Holocaust and the other horrors that mark the last century represent no indictment of our narrative. These were merely abominations committed by abominable people. Apparently the reason why our perfect society is yet to be had, even with our vast and unsurpassed stockpiles of knowledge, is because we still need more knowledge. But what more knowledge we need is difficult to determine. Nevertheless, we remain convinced that only through knowledge will our redemption be had. So our obsession with generating more and more knowledge continues. We continue to devise more and more powerful technologies and methodologies with the hope of unlocking the world's last secret. But as the march of knowledge continues, so also do the devastation and destruction, the misery and peril. There is no correlation, much less any causation, between our amassing of knowledge and moral action. Yet becoming knowledgeable is to supposed to civilize us, neutralize our primal instincts and impulses. By any definition being knowledgeable is supposed to be a good thing. If so, how then do we explain the absence of any relation between our pursuit of knowledge and moral action? How much more can we continue to prop up the illusion that more knowledge will make for more prosperity? Eventually, of course, every illusion must come to terms with reality. But what will become of us as this illusion continues to play out? How much more devastation and destruction can the world endure before we are damned?

As much as we would like to believe otherwise, the Holocaust was by no means an extraordinary event. The proclivity and capacity for that kind of destruction is at the heart of our narrative. For how fundamentally different is the Holocaust from our destruction of the world's oceans, forests, lakes, and rivers? Yet in all these cases, knowledge is aplenty. The problem is that we need to believe that the Holocaust was an extraordinary event—an abomination made possible by abominable people. To frame the Holocaust this way releases us from our complicity in the making of this horror. It also protects the integrity of our narrative, thereby never threatening what we have imagined the world to be. But again, at what cost? What is the continuing cost of denying and masking our own complicity in the making of so much horror?

Violence originates in our insistence that our truth is the only truth. In a world of boundless ambiguity and mystery, certainty is an abomination. It violently forecloses on possibility. It makes communication impossible, and in so doing impedes our being vulnerable to each other. Vulnerability and possibility are inextricable and inseparable. How vulnerable we are capable of being will shape what we come to experience as possible. Certainty is a creature of the ego, a creature of us. In a world of boundless ambiguity and mystery the notion of truth serves no constructive purpose. Without certainty, what becomes the foundation of truth? What also becomes of the value and purpose of truth? The notion of truth belongs to a certain story of the world, specifically one that assumes that we are capable of commanding the world's ambiguity and mystery. In this story, the focus is on us. We alone apparently have the means to unravel everything, understand everything, know everything. Discovering the world's truths is for us and our purposes. Even though the world is laden with other life forms, everything about this story is about us. We therefore have no regard for what becomes of other species from our actions and decisions. Our own survival and prosperity is foremost. In this story the ego is driving everything. It is always being stroked and encouraged, legitimized and validated. Eventually, the ego becomes egotism, dogmatism, narcissism, individualism, ethnocentrism, fundamentalism, and nationalism. There is no regard for the concerns of others, the truths of others, the experiences of others. Our cultivation of the ego explains how notions like survival of the fittest become possible, plausible, and acceptable. The ego pervades our ethics, politics, and economics. There would be no calls for the "unleashing of market forces" without the ego, no obsession with weapons of mass destruction, no exploitation of the planet's natural resources. Now the ego is unbound, taking on all manner of forms and expressions. It pervades our theories, methodologies, and technologies. It now shapes and defines everything, subsequently corrupting and disfiguring everything.

So our own story of the world has many corrosive and destructive dimensions, all of which are constantly colluding and metastasizing. All that seems certain is that this story will implode, as every story must deal with the rigors of reality. The world will only tolerate so much of our recklessness. A world with boundless ambiguity and mystery will always be larger than us. This world will never obediently submit to our desires, impulses, and fears. It will often harshly remind us of this reality. There is no place for the ego in this world. Ego diminishes our understanding of everything. It also makes the world and us less and less, impoverishing what we are capable of learning and understanding, and ultimately diminishing what we are capable of being and becoming. This is why Jainism, Buddhism, and so many other traditions have long been warning us about the ego. Our continuing failure to heed this warning is responsible for why this abomination continues to blight the world. Vulnerability involves being able to get beyond the seduction of the ego. We are to forsake certainty for vulnerability. If possibility is bound up with us ending the ego, then our redemption resides in us recognizing ourselves in each other and the world. Only through humility and vulnerability is this possible.

CHAPTER 15

On Language and Mind

Rules of grammar and usage assist us in expressing ourselves with precision. Precision in language leads to precision in thought. If we tend to be sloppy nowadays in our arguments—and we do—one reason is surely the growing sloppiness of our language.

When opponents mock a politician's struggles with grammar, they are appealing implicitly to a shared understanding that this sloppiness is wrong. And they're right. The rules define not only our language but also ourselves. That's why so many parents over the years—including my own—have insisted that their children speak English correctly. Proper grammar, to borrow from Arthur Schlesinger, serves as our passport.

Enforcing the rules of grammar is one of the ways we teach the young that rules exist—and that their existence must be cherished and protected. That's why, for example, so many observers have drawn analogies to the rules of grammar in proposing rules for the moral calculus.

The most famous proponent of the analogy was Adam Smith. In "The Theory of the Moral Sentiments," Smith wrote: "The rules of justice may be compared to the rules of grammar; the rules of the other virtues, to the rules which critics lay down for the attainment of what is sublime and elegant in composition." His point was that the rules of grammar "are precise, accurate, and indispensable," and the rules of composition "loose, vague, and indeterminate." Morality should be modeled on grammar, he argued, so that we may have *"certain and infallible directions for acquiring it."*

The theory works only if our rules are indeed "precise, accurate, and indispensable." One way of keeping our expression precise and accurate is to keep our adverbs, adverbs.

Stephen Carter, Yale University (2012)

WE CONTINUE TO BELIEVE THAT language is foundational to the development of mind. It is both constitutive and reflective of mind. Presumably, a rigorous language makes for a rigorous mind, and a rigorous mind uses language sophisticatedly, precisely, and abstractly. This is why every standardized test includes a language component. The size of our vocabulary supposedly reflects the power of our minds. This is of our popular theory of mind—language is reflective and constitutive of mind. Great civilizations are supposedly born of great languages, which means that such civilizations are institutionally obligated to protect the integrity of these great languages. To do so is to protect our minds, the very minds that supposedly made for these great civilizations.

Our of theory of mind comes the popular belief that our minds are unequal because our languages are unequal, and our civilizations are unequal because our languages are unequal. So besides being institutionally obligated to protect supposedly great languages from being corrupted and polluted, a great civilization is also institutionally obligated to promote and use only these languages. This involves devaluing, diminishing, and impeding the spread of what we view as inferior languages. It also means controlling the entry of people into our civilization who use these inferior languages, and insisting that those who do gain entry adopt our supposedly great language. Our popular theory of mind, besides shaping educational policy, also shapes national policy. In fact, our popular theory of mind influences every facet of western/European civilization. It forms the bedrock of our belief in our own civilizational superiority—superior civilizations are presumably born of superior minds, which in turn are born of superior languages. Our theory of mind shows well the inextricable relationship between theory and ideology.

It cultivates a certain set of beliefs, values, fears, and hopes. It is also foundational to the organization of our society, including shaping how resources are allocated and to whom. That every standardized test has a language component, and that these tests play an integral role in our assessing, sorting, and ranking of each other, means that this theory of mind is foundational in determining who gets what resources and opportunities. Ideologies are self-fulfilling, self-legitimizing, and self-perpetuating. What we believe influences how we perceive and experience things, and what things we value and promote reinforce what we believe. Such is the insidious nature of any ideology.

But where is the proof of this theory of mind that controls everything? That is, where is the proof that great languages have made for great minds, which have in turn made for great civilizations? Where are these great civilizations that are proof of great minds, great languages? Western/European civilization is supposedly a great civilization, even seen by most as the greatest civilization. No other civilization has apparently made as much progress, or has given the world as many books, or has made as much science and technology. But on the other hand, what other civilization is responsible for as much death and destruction, or responsible for as much ecological destruction and devastation? How could any civilization responsible for as much peril and misery be defined as great? What kind of great mind is responsible for creating such a civilization? Or, what kind of mind does such a civilization produce?

We have put language in the service of ideology. Our theory of mind is about us justifying our conquest and colonization of others. It is ideology masquerading as theory, politics masquerading as knowledge. Indeed, theory is nothing but ideology, meaning no theory comes out of an ideological vacuum. Theories do the bidding of ideologies. Such is what our popular theory of mind is doing. It is born out of our need to legitimize our belief in our supposed superiority—a superiority that allows us to coercively impose our will on the world and others.

We need a new theory of mind because the world desperately needs a new theory of mind. The world can bear only so much devastation and destruction at our hands. However, before we can arrive at that new theory of mind, we have to arrive at a new theory of language, and before we can arrive at a new theory of language, we have to arrive at a new ideology—that is, a new story of what being human means. Our popular theory of mind assumes that we are a symbolic and linguistic species, and the origins of language reside in evolutionary necessity. Presumably, language is a tool that allows us to perform various tasks that are vital for our survival and prosperity. The development of mind is supposedly achieved through the mastery of this tool. A highly complex tool supposedly makes strenuous demands on the mind in order to achieve mastery. However, if language is an evolved tool, why are linguists and anthropologists yet to find a pre-evolved language? How did all languages come to have what linguists refer to as a Universal Grammar—a common system of underlying rules and structures? No doubt, language allows us to perform highly complex tasks. It also enables coordination and organization. But how did this become the story of language? In fact, how did Charles Darwin's theory of evolution become the story of being human? To view language as a tool is to view language as a process that involves much learning. Only through intensive training is mastery of this tool eventually achieved. Supposedly, the purpose of language is to help us convey information to each other. It is fundamentally an informational phenomenon. But the problem with this theory of language (and communication) is that language is inherently metaphorical. It is always laden with metaphors. That language is inherently metaphorical means that language is inherently ideological. It also means that language is inherently ecological. That language can change and evolve also means that language can devolve and die. But language is only ecological because we are inherently ecological. We too are either evolving and flourishing or devolving and dying. Consequently, what should concern us most is how to embody language in ways that help us to evolve and flourish. What would that kind of embodying look like? What would such embodying demand of us?

To view language as a tool assumes that our own humanity is separate and outside the humanity of others. It is language that supposedly gives us the ability to share our thoughts and emotions with each other. This is supposedly how language unites us. It creates a bridge between us. This bridge facilitates the movement of our thoughts and emotions. In this theory of language, language possesses no moral dimension. It is merely a tool. How and to what ends we choose to use this tool supposedly has no bearing on the world. Evolution merely requires us to be proficient. But to view language as an ecological phenomenon is to recognize that language is moral. There are consequences that bear upon the world as a result of how we embody language. To impede the evolution of language is to impede our own moral evolution. Indeed, to view language ecologically is to recognize that my humanity is bound up with your humanity. How I embody language bears upon the condition of my humanity just as much as yours. The consequences are always ecological. Because language is ecological, mind is ecological. Mind emerges from how we embody language and also from how others embody language around us. To speak about how we embody language is to speak about what kinds of metaphors we bring to language, and the ideologies that supply us with these metaphors. In other words, besides being ecological, mind is also metaphorical. The metaphors that shape language also shape our minds. Metaphors matter. There are metaphors that enlarge how we conceptualize and experience things, and others that diminish such processes. All metaphors are by no means morally, ecologically, and epistemologically equal. The ideologies that supply us with our metaphors also matter in terms of shaping our minds. That mind is metaphorical also means that mind is ideological. Our minds are shaped by what we believe, assume, value, and fear. Just as much as there are ideologies that challenge and enlarge our minds, there are others that do differently. Mind is shaped by many forces. It is metaphorical, ideological, and ecological. Our minds can be shaped in many different ways. We can always change and evolve, learn and grow. But in order for this kind of positive process to occur, we have to promote only those ecologies and ideologies that will challenge our minds. Also, the fact that mind is metaphorical, ideological, and ecological also means that mind is emotional, sensual, sexual, relational, and spiritual. Various metaphors show this well by stimulating every dimension of our being.

Our popular theory of mind would have us believe that language is fundamentally a cognitive process. We are cultured to experience language as a cerebral activity. We are pressured to use language concisely and precisely. To use language precisely supposedly reflects a disciplined and cultured mind. Such a mind is supposedly in no way susceptible to emotions and passions, the premise again being that language is a tool that allows us to perform various vital tasks. If we are to perform such tasks effectively, which evolution supposedly requires, then language should function precisely. But all of this makes for a debilitative relation to language. We embody a language rather than merely speak a language. Reducing language to a mental activity detaches us from language. Language becomes something functional rather than something moral, something we speak rather than embody.

In our popular theory of mind, metaphors are a problem. Metaphors supposedly promote ambiguity, and as a result, invite chaos and confusion. Yet this promoting of ambiguity is exactly what makes metaphors enlivening. Lush metaphors are always throwing us into different worlds, challenging us to always look at the world anew. Without metaphors we would be bound to static and mechanistic worlds. Diversity would be impossible. What then becomes of our minds when we strive to expunge metaphors from language for the sake of functionality? How would we imagine the world anew without metaphors? But again, for the sake of functionality, we deemphasize metaphors and anything else that could hinder precision and clarity. We believe that precision, besides being necessary for accomplishing certain vital tasks, is also good for the development of the mind. It focuses and disciplines the mind, and such minds presumably make for great civilizations. Such again is the story of our theory of mind. Strong languages supposedly make for strong minds, which in turn make for strong civilizations, and which in turn make for strong minds. But with so much devastation and destruction at the hands of our own supposedly great civilization, how could the mind that made such a civilization be seen as great? How also could the language that made for such a mind be defined as great? Put differently, only an impoverished mind could produce a civilization that is responsible for so much death and destruction, misery and peril. So how did our minds become so impoverished?

How did our language become so impoverished? Indeed, how did we become so impoverished, as seen by our willingness to destroy our own habitat? Possibly the impoverishment began in language, with us reducing language to something functional and mechanical rather than something spiritual and epistemological.

The Bible begins with the announcement that first there was the Word and the Word was God—that is, God brought the world into being through language. God resides in language. Such is the power of language. Such is what language is capable of doing. Such is what language gives us the power to do. How did language come to lose this magnificent power? How did we become complicit in our own impoverishment? But the price of our impoverishment is now upon us. Rather than creating worlds we are now destroying worlds with how we embody language.

We can theorize plenty about how and where the deterioration of our relation to language began. But we do know that oral-based languages have many distinct life-affirming attributes. For instance, according to Walter Ong, "writing fosters abstractions that disengage knowledge from the [environment] where human beings struggle with one another. It separates the knower and known. On the other hand, by keeping knowledge embedded in the life world, orality situates knowledge within a context of struggle." Also, "primary orality fosters personality structures that in certain ways are more communal and externalized, and less introspective than those common among literates. Oral communication unites people in groups. Writing and reading are solitary activities that throw the psyche back on itself." We also know that our conquest of others had a lot to do with the invention and propagation of writing-based languages. Bureaucracy is a creature of writing. In turn, bureaucracy produces alienation by cultivating submission, subordination, and repetition. It achieves conformity through fear. It takes away our ability to act boldly, courageously, and imaginatively. Bureaucracy succeeds by taking away everything that makes us human. Our sacred relation to language is lost as bureaucracy stresses functionality. Language must be devoid of ambiguity and complexity so as to avoid chaos and confusion. In other words, language must be devoid of ambiguity and complexity so that instructions and regulations could move smoothly throughout the bureaucracy. So bureaucracy comes into being as a result of our alienation from language, and in turn promotes our own alienation by distancing us from language. In becoming self-perpetuating, bureaucracy also becomes self-negating. As such, the expansion of bureaucracy is inevitable. As we become more and more alienated, bureaucratized, and institutionalized, we need more and more rules and structures to function. Our dependency on bureaucracy deepens. We eventually even lose the ability to imagine the world without bureaucracy.

But most troubling is how bureaucracy destroys our minds. The fear that comes with all the normalizing and conforming pressures corrodes the mind. It discourages vulnerability, as in our fear to embody language honestly and courageously—to speak our truths on our terms and conditions. Such fear can also be seen in our fear of conflict, in our fear of offending others, in our fear to trust others, to commit to others, to love others. Indeed, such fear can be amply seen in our endless deception, deceit, and duplicity. Such is now the fear that shapes our minds. Of course, no mind that is laden with such fear can produce anything extraordinary.

Our popular theory of mind makes no mention of fear. Mind is presumably shaped by biology and constitutes our psychology. This is why we continue to believe that the ability and potentiality of our minds can be reliably measured and quantified. Sociology, anthropology, communicology, and theology supposedly have nothing much to do with the shaping of our minds. But increasingly the world is revealing to us that biology, sociology, psychology, anthropology, and communicology are all bound up with each other. This is why mind is ecological. It is also why bureaucracy has a corrosive and debilitative effect on the mind. On the other hand, bureaucracy is also a creature of corrosive and debilitative minds. It is also attractive to such minds. Weak minds demand conformity, stability, and homogeneity. Such minds make for a certain kind of ideology, which in turn make for a certain kind of society, one that is deeply bureaucratized and institutionalized. We need both social theory and institutional theory to understand the origins of bureaucracy.

A bureaucracy institutionally cultivates a certain kind of ideology, and ideologically legitimizes that ideology. This is what makes a bureaucracy so insidious. It produces the minds that legitimize the ideology that drives the processes that ultimately make the minds. In the end, a bureaucracy reveals how mind is a product of ecological, ideological, and institutional forces. However, besides making and encouraging a certain kind of ideology, a mind born of bureaucracy also makes for a certain kind of epistemology that also in turn corrodes the mind. In this epistemology, language is a tool. It is a tool to describe a world that is outside and separate from us. As always, the goal is to use language skillfully and precisely. Precision is the goal. We want our observations and descriptions to perfectly mirror the workings of the world. With this epistemology the goal is to use language in ways that are presumably devoid of ideology—to use language clinically and rigorously. Language should be cleansed of all emotions and passions. Metaphors must be removed. Focus is on employing various methodologies and technologies to produce pure and pristine descriptions. Presumably, such descriptions can only come from a language that is also pure and pristine. But again, in order to achieve this kind of language, language must be cleansed of all emotions and passions. Metaphors must be removed. Of course, all of this is illusory as language is inherently metaphorical. Still, what becomes of the condition of our minds through this washing and cleansing of language? How could any epistemology that impoverishes our minds by impoverishing our language possibly produce any profound observations and descriptions? We should, in fact, be in no way surprised when Thomas Kuhn concludes after studying the history of science that "No part of the aim of normal science is to call forth new sorts of phenomena; indeed those that will not fit the box are often not seen at all. Nor do scientists normally aim to invent new theories, and they are often intolerant of those invented by others. Instead, normal-scientific research is directed to the articulation of those phenomena and theories that the paradigm already supplies."

Yet we continue to believe that great minds are unlocking the world's deepest truths. Thanks to these supposedly great minds, progress is being achieved. We are supposedly blessed to have so many great minds in our midst. We are also presumably fortunate to have various institutions of higher learning that are capable of cultivating these great minds that will produce all this great progress and prosperity. If so, however, then such great minds must also be held accountable for all the devastation and destruction, misery and peril that our civilization has produced. How could great minds be complicit in doing something that no other species will do—destroy their own habitat? What kind of great mind would do something that even an ant would never do? Nevertheless, our obsession with identifying and ultimately cultivating great minds continues. We are no less obsessed in upholding and privileging the great institutions of higher learning that will harness the great minds that will eventually become captains of science, industry, and politics. We will never forget to mention the great education that these institutions offer. But again, how could any education be defined as great that is fully complicit in so much death and destruction?

We define a great education as first and foremost rigorous. It disciplines the mind. It makes the mind rational, analytical, and computational. A great education fosters restraint. It allows us to control our emotions and passions through the building of strong minds. But apparently only few of us have the potential to be truly great minds. It will be the select few that will receive a great education from our supposedly great institutions of higher learning. We also believe that our commitment to building great minds is what is responsible for our unsurpassed greatness. In the end, a great education is supposedly both demanding and challenging. The goal is to give the mind a certain shape and sculpture. We are seeking to chisel away those proclivities and tendencies that weaken the mind. Language training is presumably vital to this mission. A supposedly great education is characterized by much reading and writing. We demand that students read the great books by the great minds of our civilization. We also expect a lot of rigorous writing that employs all the protocols of argumentation and persuasion. Outside of the classroom we encourage debate, chess, and other cerebral games that presumably help discipline the mind. In giving us the ability to control our passions and emotions, a great education assumes that the cultivation of a great mind makes us moral. A moral person is rational, analytical, and computational, meaning that the supposed greatness of our own civilization is a reflection of our own moral superiority. Being educationally great makes us scientifically, technologically, economically great, but ultimately morally great. This is the story of our popular theory of mind. Our theory of mind apparently just happens to perfectly explain our own supposed greatness. This is another example of how theory and ideology draw upon each other to protect the status quo. We also have theory and ideology working in tandem to promote and legitimize various structures and institutions that further protect the status quo. Affecting any kind of profound change is all but impossible. This is also how a hegemony comes into being, through the weaving of ideological, epistemological, and institutional practices.

Besides a new ideology and a new epistemology, a new theory of mind also needs a new pedagogy that values the relationship between mind and body, mind and spirit, mind and heart, mind and environment, and mind and relationships. Attending to the mind involves attending to all these relationships. An impoverished mind speaks to the impoverishment of all these relationships. Our popular theory of mind has left us emotionally, existentially, sensually, and spiritually impoverished. Our rampant devastation and destruction could have all been predicted. With all our great minds, our great institutions of learning, we can make no claim of being morally superior to ants. For when did ants ever put other ants in servitude and bondage, or sent other ants to death camps? Yet our popular theory of mind claims that we are morally superior to ants because we have an evolved (superior) linguistic and symbolic capacity that facilitates superior kinds of cognitive processes, such as abstract thought. The carnage that surrounds us plainly reveals that this theory makes no sense. Still, this theory of mind continues to torment native and indigenous peoples. This theory guides developmental aid projects in many native and indigenous cultures. It is seen in the focus on promoting formal education and building schools.

Formal education is presumably the path to progress and prosperity. It will save us from our own backwardness. In addition to enhancing our material resources, formal (bureaucratized) education will expand our moral resources. We will supposedly become less tribal and less a threat to each other. Ideally, education promises to make us global citizens. To become so morally evolved is to have no regards for race, ethnicity, nationality, and country. These things are supposedly the creatures of our emotions and passions, instincts and impulses. Our own civilizational superiority can supposedly be seen in our commitment to a global politics and economics that will better all of humankind. Our great institutions of higher learning teem with all manner of international studies programs. Our students are encouraged to "think globally, act locally." All of this speaks to our supposed moral superiority, thanks to our investment in building great minds. Apparently, no other civilization has a comparable commitment to improving the condition of all humankind. We view ourselves as on the cusp of vanquishing the final vestiges of our own tribalism. But our enormous appetite for war belies this claim. Moreover, our unsurpassed stockpiles of weapons of mass destruction, as well as our proliferation of these weapons, makes a mockery of the claim that we are committed to the well-being of all humankind. Our own plundering of the world's natural resources for our own selfish gain also undermines this claim.

Our theory of mind makes for a pedagogy that impoverishes us intellectually, morally, and spiritually. This pedagogy assumes that affairs of the heart, the body, the spirit, the environment have nothing to do with learning. It defines learning in terms of proficiency and competency. Learning can be measured, evaluated, and even quantified. But what to make of all this learning that is supposedly happening in our great institutions of higher learning? Where is the correlation between all this learning and our own moral development? That is, where is the proof that all our unsurpassed learning is making us morally superior? Or, what is the worth of any learning that is encouraging us to destroy our own habitat? But as the promotion of formal education spreads throughout the world, this will be the pedagogy and model of learning that will be soon consuming the world. Such is the insidious nature of colonialism.

CHAPTER 16
ON THE LIMITS OF THEORY

ANY THEORY THAT PROFESSES TO explain the order of the world should be magnificent. We should be in awe of what the theory will never be able to explain rather than what it professes to explain. This, for instance, is the problem with Darwin's theory of evolution. It lacks magnificence. It would have us believe that we are capable of explaining the order of life, and even capable of doing so definitively. There is no awe. But how could we look into the heavens and profess to know the origins of life? How does one arrive at such hubris? No doubt, if we can explain the origins of life, then surely we can explain everything else. In this case hubris means that our capacity to do all these things makes us special. For what other species can presumably explain the nature and origins of life, or have devised the means to study the heavens?

We also continue to assume that our theories are merely objectively describing a world that is separate and outside from us. In other words, our theories are supposedly devoid of ideologies. In this way our theories serve a vital ideological function, allowing us to believe that we are special and superior to other civilizations that presumably have no theories. For what other civilizations presumably have theorists comparable to Darwin and Einstein? Where are such theorists in our textbooks? The validity of our theories is secondary. What really matters is that our theories make us believe we are superior. That we alone are apparently capable of theorizing about the nature and origins of life means that we are superior to all other species and civilizations. Our theories legitimize our power to rule the world. Consequently, every theory comes laden with hubris, always promising to explain definitively. We are even working on a theory that will definitively explain everything. Yes, the theory of everything. No theory gets any prize for humility. We remain convinced that our theories are objectively and accurately describing and explaining a world that is separate and outside of us. We apparently have no choice but to heed these descriptions and observations. It is, again, the ideological function of the theory that really matters. Our theories legitimize what we imagine the world to be. Our theories lack magnificence because we lack the courage to imagine the world in bold new ways. Or, simply put, our theories mask our cowardice. We are afraid, deeply and terribly afraid. We are nothing but organic beings in a boundless world. There is nothing that speaks compellingly to our importance and relevance as a species. For what does our existence have to do with the need for billions of planets? What to make of our own belief of nothing else being out there? There is also nothing that definitively speaks to our superiority. For what other species (and civilization) is responsible for as much death and destruction? What other species (and civilization) is responsible for putting the planet in such peril? In sum, what is the value of our theories?

Before theories there were stories. In fact, most civilizations still only have stories. But with modernity came the rise of theories and the demise of stories. Theories supposedly represent progress, thereby representing the rise of reason, rigor, reason, and precision. But most of all, theories presumably represent our dominion over the world. In describing how the world works, theories presumably allow us to control how the world works. This, again, is how theories give us dominion over the world, or the impression of such. However, in order for our theories to perform this vital ideological function, the invention of various illusions becomes necessary. We have to believe that our own capacity to describe the world is special and superior. We also have to believe that the world's mystery will kneel to our theories and methodologies. Finally, we have to believe that our conquering of the world's mystery is the path to prosperity. Without out theories and a commitment to building final theories, we will supposedly descend into anarchy and prosperity will elude us. Thus, if progress and prosperity are to be had, theories are supposedly necessary. We therefore need to believe that our theories have been making for a kind of prosperity and progress that nothing else could afford, much less match.

But what to do now when such progress and prosperity continue to bring death and destruction, misery and despair? How can there be no indictment of our theories and our obsession with theories? But the fault cannot be entirely put at the feet of theory. We will always be in the theory business. Any investigation that begins with why and how is about theory. The problem is with all the modernist illusions that shape how we engage and frame theory. That is, the problem is with the ideology that shapes and situates the doing of theory. We are aspiring to have theory do something that is simply impossible—to give the impression that we are capable of conquering the world's boundless mystery. In a world of boundless mystery, no theory can do such a thing. In such a world all theory can allow us to do is explore, speculate, and conjecture. Yet this is where and how theory is most valuable. But to approach theory this way demands a certain kind of ideological and epistemological humility. It must begin in our worldview. This kind of humility is alien to us because this kind of worldview is alien to us. We demand a definitive knowledge because we believe that we are capable of arriving at such a knowledge, because we are an inherently superior species. Using theory to achieve certainty becomes inevitable. Yet how could certainty be possible in a world of boundless mystery? What manner of illusions makes this even seemingly reasonable? But because our goal is certainty, our mission is to test and test until certainty—as seen by the ability of the theory to predict accurately—is had. We then excitedly announce the new theory to the world, to once again show off our dominion over the world and our civilizational superiority.

The announcement of every new theory serves to validate our progress and prosperity, especially the epistemology that is making all of this possible. However, the endless testing actually guarantees that the theory will achieve the desired certainty. To test a theory already involves assuming what a theory is assuming. So to test a theory about angels involves assuming the possibility of angels. There must be agreement between what the theory is describing and the world that is being described. Through testing this agreement inevitably converges, as the theory is bound by measures of proof that must also be in agreement with what the theory is assuming and the world that is being assumed. Again, how can we test a theory of angels against a world where there is no conception of angels? What would be the measure of proof and from which worldview would such measure be taken? Testing a theory is really about affirming the world that is being assumed. Just as much as no theory can violate the world from which it is born, no test can violate the world from which it is born. By cultivating agreement between the theory and the world the theory is assuming, testing guarantees certainty. This is how theory seemingly makes for a definitive and accumulative knowledge, meaning this is how theory does the bidding of ideology. But this is also how theory works against us. For what is the value of any theory that can only legitimize and concretize the world we are ready and willing to imagine? How much can any such theory do for us? How does such a theory enrich the human experience? In fact, how does any such theory enlarge our sense of what is possible?

All of this raises a fundamental question—what should theory be for? We are, of course, supposed to frown upon prescriptive questions? Who, after all, should possess the power to declare what should be the purpose of theory? But the fact remains that theory can do different things, and these things come with different consequences. In the end, consequences matter. Thus asking questions about the purpose of theory is both valid and valuable. This kind of inquiry in no way assumes that there is a final answer to these kinds of questions. It merely assumes the possibility of theory being something different, meaning the possibility of a different relationship between theory and us. But of course this possibility begins with us, specifically our willingness to have a different relationship with theory. This involves being ready and willing to have a different relationship with the world, as in being ready to accept the fact that theory will always float on an ocean of boundless mystery. There will always be doubt, ambiguity, and confusion. Even our best theories will always remind us of our smallness. So coming to a new relationship with theory begins with locating theory in a new moral, ideological, and epistemological setting.

In addition to possessing ideological and epistemological dimensions, theories also have sensual, emotional, and spiritual dimensions. When a theory affirms our world this poses no kind of sensual, emotional, and spiritual risks to us. The body is excused from the doing of theory. In other words, the doing of theory poses no challenge to what the body feels and senses. There is no demand for the evolution of new states of being. We are spared the angst that comes with such evolution. The doing of theory becomes merely a mental exercise, or at least this is our impression. This impression is further legitimized by our own belief that mind and body are different things. But this impression is false, as the doing of theory involves metaphors, and our metaphors come from our sensual, emotional, historical, and ideological selves. Mind is always bound up with the body, which means that expressions of mind are also expressions of the body. It also means that theory development involves expansion of the body. Our theories are impoverished because our bodies are impoverished.

Looking at theory anew and repurposing theory involves expanding what we are capable of sensing, believing, and experiencing. Notions of love, empathy, compassion, mercy, generosity, kindness, and tenderness are vital to theory development. What we are capable of perceiving, grasping, and understanding is bound up with what we are capable of sensing, believing, and experiencing. Mind is as much body as body is mind. To theorize is to enlarge our sense of being, to challenge the limits of what we are capable of understanding. This is why even our best theories will always be incomplete. We can always push further the forces that limit our sense of being. We do so through compassion, mercy, love, generosity, and tenderness. Enlarging our ability to do all of these things is what theory development requires of us. This is how our theories become magnificent. Our theories become magnificent by us becoming magnificent. Such is what comes from pushing against the limits of what and who we are capable of loving and forgiving. We become magnificent. We realize our beauty and potentiality. Humility falls upon us. We lose the egotism, and subsequently the narcissism and ethnocentrism, that violently impedes what we are capable of perceiving, experiencing, and understanding. We become less primal, less obsessed with our own survival and self-interest. Theorizing is both a moral and spiritual undertaking. A valuable theory enlarges our sense of possibility by creating and opening new vistas of what we are capable of being and becoming.

But because consequences matter, our impoverished theories come with a price. By legitimizing and concretizing worlds that are creatures of our morally and spiritually impoverished selves, these theories achieve a kind of supremacy that is difficult to disrupt. The ideological environs favor these theories as much as these theories favor the environs. As such, these theories always seem to be accurately describing the world. In many ways these theories become all but infallible and eventually begin to shape every facet of our lives. We cannot imagine the world outside of these theories. These theories simply seem to make a kind of intuitive sense, to really describe a world that is outside of us, rather than one born of our imagination or lack thereof.

CHAPTER 17
On The End of Truth

How could there be a notion like truth in a world that is so phenomenally vast and boundless? Or put differently, what made for the invention of this notion? Truth assumes certainty. This is why gravity is seen as a truth. All things fall to the ground. Truth also assumes a complete understanding of something. It requires and promotes a conviction of certainty, as in knowing for certain an object will fall to the ground when pushed off a table. But how could such certainty be possible or even useful in a world so unbelievably vast? Yes, all things will fall to the ground. But in a world with billions of planets and possibly many universes, how valuable is this truth?

Truth diminishes us. It encourages us to focus on only those things that we are capable of understanding completely, or those things that make for that kind of illusion. We also tend to perceive the world in ways that make this notion credible and important. So yes, objects do fall to the ground. But how does this truth make for a world with less misery and suffering? Also, what of the divisive nature of truth? That is, what about how truth promotes division and separation? Truth is supposedly something we can possess. However, if one side has the truth, then what the other side has is false. Presumably, truth has a certain character. That I can supposedly possess it means that it conforms to a certain perception and expectation. I must be able to announce that this is truth. Anything else is false. This is how truth divides the world into that which is true and that which is false. But this is only the beginning of the separation and division. The truth is nearly always good, just, and moral. To have the truth is to have something good and valuable. Truth brings good things into the world. What could be the possibility of order, progress, and civilization without truth? On the other hand, what becomes of the side that presumably possesses falsehoods, and thereby the things that presumably undermine order, progress, and civilization? How can we mutually coexist with this side or in any way help this side thrive? The side that supposedly possesses the truth seems obligated to denounce the other side and let the world know which side possesses the truth. What is the other side to do but denounce the other side? This is how truth puts us at each other's throats. To possess the truth is presumably to have that which is superior, meaning that to possess the truth makes us superior to those we perceive as possessing falsehoods. Truth legitimizes us and distinguishes our actions and decisions. In a world that believes in truth, diversity is impossible as those who are different can never be our moral equals.

Truth is an ideological device. Its purpose is to help us believe that we are capable of conquering the world's vastness. We really have no interest in truth per se. What really matters is the illusion of truth, or what truth allows us to believe. We have long been in the truth business as truth is seductive. Truth supposedly stands outside of time and space. This is why it is always "hard" and enduring. The purpose of truth is to magnify our capacity. Truth proclaims that we are in no way at the mercy of the world's vastness. This is arguably why both science and religion are in the truth business. Both would like us to believe that each is fundamentally different from the other. But both are staunchly in the truth business. Both are fundamentally using truth to change our relationship with the world's vastness. Neither is willing to accept that the world's vastness is unconquerable. To accept this reality—even this truth—would change everything, beginning with how we define and relate to knowledge.

To believe in truth is to believe that our redemption resides in knowledge, and in how much knowledge we can acquire. Our pursuit is unrelenting as apparently no amount of truth is enough. Yet we have only been in the truth business on paper. What we believe will always shape how we perceive and make sense of the world, meaning that the relationship between ontology and epistemology is inviolable. Truth is a reflection of belief. What we perceive to be true is what we believe to be true. Ontology is bound up with epistemology. Yet both religion and science would like us to believe that ontology and epistemology are outside and separate of each other. In the case of religion there are supposed truths that come to us directly from God. In the case of science there are supposed truths that our methods have consistently shown to be true. Indeed, certain truths may no doubt be divine, but how we came to value and perceive these truths as divine can be found with what we believe the world to be. In other words, every truth belongs to a narrative. A worldview is a narrative. It is a story of how the world is and needs to be. We are narrative beings. Through narratives we perceive and make sense of things.

Our narratives shape what truths we perceive and value. Yet every narrative begins with an ontology—something we believe and need to believe. Ontology makes our narratives fallible and vulnerable. Neither religion nor science wants us to own this fallibility and vulnerability as doing so would mean fundamentally changing our relationship with the world's vastness. We would have to release ourselves of the ambition of trying to conquer the world's vastness and believing that even doing so is possible. We would eventually recognize that even this ambition is a creature of a narrative. There is no spiritual or existential imperative that makes this ambition inevitable. It is purely ideological. But finally, we would come to recognize that this quest to conquer the world's vastness has been enormously destructive. It impedes diversity by undermining the kind of epistemological humility that is vital for us to have to be vulnerable to different positions and experiences. If we genuinely believe that we possess the truth, how vulnerable can we be to the supposed truths of others? Truth makes communication impossible. Persuasion becomes inevitable as all that remains is the impulse to impose our truths upon others by any available means. The goal is conversion, to have others adopt our truths, our positions, our perceptions, and ultimately our values, norms, beliefs, and expectations. In other words, the goal is to homogenize by degrading, undermining, and displacing the truths of others.

So what is the origin of communication? Communication studies claims that the origins of communication can be found in evolutionary necessity, specifically in our need to share and exchange information for purposes of achieving superior levels of organization and coordination. As such, persuasion is presumably a kind of communication. In us being supposedly nothing but bundles of selfish genes, persuasion is presumably about us using communication to achieve our own evolutionary goals and objectives. Persuasion (presumably) politicizes communication. It puts communication in the service of ideology, specifically the ideology that favors our own interests. In our popular story of communication, persuasion is both inevitable and necessary. In fact, many within communication studies claim that all communication is persuasional, a struggle over competing and conflicting interests. We prevail by commanding and employing the most effective persuasional techniques. Thus communication is most commonly defined as an art form, and proficiency is measured in terms of commanding various skills and techniques. The popular view is that rhetoric (the study of persuasion) elevates the study of communication by locating communication within the political and ideological realm. It supposedly moves the study of communication away from the realm of the biological, relational, and cultural. But what do we make of rhetorical theory's hostility to diversity? What to make of the consequences and implications that come from this unrelenting hostility?

To believe in truth is to have little regard for consequences and implications. Truth means that certain consequences and implications are simply inevitable. No doubt, certain consequences and implications can be ameliorated. But why? If a truth is that which evolution rewards for being the strongest, brightest, and fittest, why should those who are supposedly so be discouraged from exploiting those who are supposedly weak, dumb, and lazy? Such an intervention would seem comparable to trying to make a mango tree produce plums. Truth assumes that human beings have no capacity to do anything profound. We are either bundles of selfish genes, or beings who are born of sin and must obediently submit to an authoritarian God. Either way, our redemption supposedly depends on us abiding or submitting to a certain set of truths. We supposedly violate these truths at our own peril. Evidently, truth domesticates us. It promotes submission. On the other hand, many would claim that the search for truth promotes exploration rather than submission. But what of our submission to all the protocols, regulations, and methods of science that make the formation of fundamentally new truths impossible? This was Thomas Kuhn's contribution, that science has no interest in the discovery of new truths. Yet we continue to profess that we are committed to the truth and valuing nothing but the truth. But who has any interests in things that are false? And things are false only because other things are cast as true. However, how did this binary become our only option? Where is this written in stone? Most importantly, how valuable is this binary of truth and falsehood? That this kind of question is even possible makes plain that the world is by no means bound to the notion of truth. What of possibility?

Instead of asking whether something is true or false, we could ask questions about possibility, such as what does a certain course of action make possible, or how can we enlarge what outcomes are possible? Possibility changes our relationship with the world's vastness. It pulls us towards this vastness by inviting us to explore the limits of our own potentiality. So instead of arguing over which religions are true or false, a much more heuristic way of looking at our religious diversity is in terms of each religion presenting a different relation and definition of God. Thus Judaism offers a certain kind of possibility, Buddhism another, Hinduism another, and so forth. All possible relations and interpretations are by no means morally equal. On the other hand, no possibility is ever complete and absolute. For possibility means context, as in this context, this is possible. As our contexts change, so also what becomes possible changes. We have the ability to enlarge what is possible by pushing against the legitimacy of the forces that make for different contexts.

Whether our story of communication is true or false is irrelevant. What is much more heuristic is asking what makes us amenable to this story and what kind of world does this story make possible. To believe that the origin of communication resides in evolutionary necessity is to believe that persuasion is the goal of communication. We benefit by getting others to adopt our view of the world. Persuasion also presumably saves us the costs and risks of using other means to impose our will upon others. From an evolutionary standpoint, persuasion is efficient. We can make others submit to our will without firing a shot. In this way, persuasion is supposedly a hallmark of evolutionary fitness. But in terms of possibility, this story is devoid of value and purchase. This story promotes a definition of communication that impedes diversity, meaning this is a story of communication that wants nothing to do with communication. Communication means possibility, as in the possibility of a new meaning, a new understanding, a new interpretation, a new relationship. Without communication all of these things are impossible. We would be devoid of any means to use the world's vastness to expand our worlds through the generation of new meanings, new interpretations, and so forth. So without being able to generate new meanings, new understandings, new interpretations, and so forth, diversity is impossible.

This is how communication is bound up with diversity. This is how possibility is bound up with diversity. This is how possibility is bound up with life. This is how communication is bound up with life. Every new meaning, every new understanding, reminds us that the world's vastness is boundless. We will never arrive at a meaning that can encompass this vastness. But this is the origin of so much of our misery—our belief that we have a meaning that can encompass this vastness. We have no interest in generating or listening to a new meaning, a new understanding, a new interpretation. We are convinced that our truth is the only truth. Simply put, the origin of human misery begins when communication ends. For again, what is the possibility of communication when I am convinced that my truth is the only truth? What reason or incentive do I have to listen to the supposed truths of others? To honestly listen to the truths of others requires that I be open to the possibility that my own truth is fallible, which involves owning my own fallibility. It is also about recognizing that much of my fallibility comes from the fact that the world's vastness is unconquerable. So at the most fundamental level communication saves us from a lot of death and misery. It also brings diversity, as in the possibility of new meanings and understandings, into the world. But probably most importantly, communication enlarges us mentally, emotionally, existentially, and spiritually by pressing us against the world's vastness. Through the constant creation of new meanings, new interpretations, new understandings, and new relationships, we are born anew. This is how communication constitutes a life-affirming process. It stretches and enlarges every dimension of our being by keeping us at the center of the world's vastness where nothing can remain stable and complete.

In communication there is no arriving at, no coming to a shared meaning, no converging of minds, no coming to a common understanding. These kinds of homogenizing processes reflect a definition of communication that assumes that diversity impedes communication. We are to assume that diversity and communication are different things. We are also to assume that communication helps with the managing of diversity by helping us understand our differences. After all, a tool helps us to perform an important task. In this case, the task is to help us manage our differences as failure to do so effectively will supposedly make for chaos. But how exactly did diversity and communication come to be different things? Presumably, diversity is about race, gender, ethnicity, sexuality, disability, and other such differences that reside outside of communication. But this popular story of diversity is as morally impoverished as our popular story of communication. We have no interest in promoting diversity. What passes for the promotion of diversity is really the promotion of homogeneity. In this story of diversity, diversity can only be included, and in order for inclusion to occur, diversity must be assimilated. It must be stripped of any and every thing that poses a threat to the status quo. The demands of inclusion guarantee that diversity will pose no threat to the status quo. What then is the value of this diversity? What is the possibility of new meanings, new interpretations, new understandings, without the possibility of disrupting the status quo? The status quo reflects what meanings, understandings, and relationships are tolerated, encouraged, and nurtured, and which others will be excluded, discouraged, and harassed. We are to assume that the world only allows for a certain set of meanings, and such meanings can be acquired by us through the use of various methods and techniques. We devote a lot of attention to developing these methods and techniques.

CHAPTER 18

ON THE POLITICS OF DIVERSITY

So WHAT HAPPENS AFTER DIVERSITY has been marginalized, persecuted, and forsaken? That is, what happens after diversity decides to be diversity and suffer the wrath, the contempt, and the scorn that come with rejecting the status quo? How should I conduct myself when dealing with those who perceive and judge me as being inferior and a threat to all that is good, decent, and excellent? How do I handle all the pretense, hypocrisy, and deceit? What should I do in the face of all the attempts to publicly humiliate me? What could come from expressing all my rage when I know that futility abounds? Still, something has to be done with the rage that could turn ordinary human beings into beasts. This is the story of diversity. It never ends well. In the face of this reality, what must diversity do? What becomes of the ethics and politics of diversity? What must I do with the rage?

The rage will probably never go away. The cruelties and absurdities are impossible to avoid. Even Jesus Christ struggled with taming the rage. But what can the rest of us do to contain the rage? How do we release ourselves of all the violent and destructive passions? This is the politics of diversity—finding ways to remain human rather than merely different. It is about trying to find the most constructive ways to manage the rage that is always threatening to make us less human. The politics of diversity is about trying to keep the rage from killing us, from making us less human, from disfiguring our beauty and humanity. But such a politics cannot only be about survival and contest, resistance and perseverance. It must ultimately be a politics of affirmation. Diversity is an expression of our full humanity, our emancipation from fear. We are different because we refuse to be crippled by fear. Without courage, diversity is impossible. Diversity is about being unwilling to be afraid, as in possessing the fortitude and resolve to defy the norms, customs, and traditions that seek to homogenize and assimilate. Diversity is an expression of a certain kind of being. This, again, is why viewing diversity in terms of race, gender, sexuality, and even disability constitutes such a shallow conception of diversity and makes for a regressive politics of diversity that values inclusion rather than revolution. A politics of diversity has to be about the cultivation of those practices that make us fully human, and the eradication of those that make us less so.

But what exactly is the origin of this rage that tends to surround diversity? Does this rage really come from the slights, the hurts, and abuses that diversity encounters? This would mean that that the rage is *caused* by the doings of others. It is *caused* by forces outside of us. But this is bad psychology, and bad psychology makes for bad politics. This rage is of our own making, our own doing. We give life to this rage. We nurture this rage. This rage is born of our own egotism and narcissism, as in our privileging our own needs, desires, and ambitions. Only our diversity should supposedly concern us, or should concern us the most. But what of the condition of the diversity found in trees, plants, animals, and other organic beings? Why should only the condition of our diversity matter, and matter most? In fact, how did the condition of our diversity become separate from the diversity found in forests, oceans, and rivers? Such is the insidious nature of the ego. There would be no narcissism, racism, tribalism, and ethnocentrism, without egotism. So a politics of diversity must be about neutralizing the ego. The ego divides and separates, balkanizes and homogenizes. Diversity integrates. It makes community possible by making visible the relationships that bind us to the world and each other.

Diversity will always have to deal with all kinds of cruelties, absurdities, and hypocrisies. We become human through relationships, and fully human by sharing ourselves selflessly with others. Diversity is inherently relational, communal, and ecological. It emerges between human beings rather than something that is possessed by a human being as a result of being a certain persuasion by forces of birth. A politics of diversity needs to always remind us of this reality. Diversity exceeds us. The proclivity of the world is to promote diversity. Coming to terms with the ego requires enormous practice and discipline. We work our way through the ego by enlarging ourselves, pushing ourselves to do things that are really hard, such as forgiving and being tender with those who scheme and conspire against diversity. That such things are hard remind us that diversity is an extraordinary thing that can only come from extraordinary people.

CHAPTER 19

On The End of Violence

STEPHEN PINKER'S BOOK, *The Better Angels of Our Nature: Why Violence Has Declined*, is filled with many impressive charts, diagrams, and lists that presumably show how the western and European world has achieved the highest level of civilization by taming our violent instincts and impulses. It did so, according to Pinker (2011), by developing efficient and effective government systems and controls that protect us from others' violent whims and passions, by promoting education, by fostering a cosmopolitan view of the world, by valuing gender equality, and by cultivating reason and empathy. He credits modernity with the rise of these values, practices, and institutions, and also credits these movements for the progress that the rest of the world is now making in taming our violent instincts and impulses. Pinker defines modernity as "the transformation of human life by science, technology, and reason, with the attendant diminishment of custom, faith, community, traditional authority, and embeddedness in nature" (p. 692). Besides improving our physical and material comforts, Pinker also credits modernity for giving us access to "the higher and nobler things in life, such as knowledge, beauty, and human connection. Until recently most people never traveled more than a few miles from their place of birth. Everyone was ignorant of the vastness of the cosmos, the prehistory of civilization, the genealogy of living things, the genetic code, the microscopic world, and the constituents of matter. Musical recordings, affordable books, instant news of the world, productions of great art, and filmed dramas were inconceivable, let alone available in a tool that can fit in a shirt pocket" (p. 693).

Pinker's *The Better Angels of Our Nature* is a celebration of modernity. He assumes a narrative of progress that begins with us being primitive. We supposedly have always been morally and biologically evolving. In this regard, Pinker believes that the taming of our violent impulses was all but inevitable as violence ultimately threatens our evolutionary prosperity. This narrative of evolutionary progress, according to Pinker, can now be empirically seen in the impressive array of charts, lists, and diagrams found in *The Better Angels of Our Nature* that supposedly show a steady decline of violence over human history. Yet Pinker is only using violence as a case study. He is really trying to affirm Darwin's theory of evolution. History is presumably a story of evolution. Our progress merely reflects our genes figuring out what survival practices promote evolution and reproduction.

But how Pinker employs Darwin's theory is different from even how Darwin understood evolution. Early criticisms of Pinker's thesis point to the fact that Darwin never believed that evolution makes for any kind of moral progress. In the quest for survival each entity does what is necessary by maximizing gain and minimizing loss. However, for argument purposes, let us pretend that Pinker is in accord with Darwin's theory. Let us even pretend that, upon studying Pinker's many lists, charts, and diagrams, Darwin would have agreed with Pinker. Both Pinker and Darwin would still have a narrative of history that is civilizationally troubled. For what to make of those civilizations, like Jainism and Buddhism, that go back hundreds of years before the birth of western and European civilization, that opposed all manner of violence? There is still no philosophy or movement that equals Jainism's opposition to violence. Jainism prohibits inflicting pain and misery on any living entity. We are even to avoid walking on grass. Yes, probably the western and European world began in savagery, but to make that case for the rest of the world without making any mention of Buddhism and Jainism is a serious problem. From the perspective of Jainism and Buddhism, the world is actually morally devolving. In sum, Pinker makes no case that all of the world is morally progressing as a result of the rise of modernity. Jainism and Buddhism make plain that the world has long possessed conceptual and ideological systems to end our violent passions and impulses. There is also no case to be made that modernism is conceptually superior to Jainism and Buddhism in meeting this mission. In fact, Jainism and Buddhism give us much more expansive conceptions of violence by showing how our violence upon each other is related to our violence upon the planet. Modernism gives us no such connection, and as a result, gives us no way to fully understand the consequences of our ecological destructiveness. For as much as the amount of violence inflicted upon persons is probably decreasing in the western world, what cannot be missed are our increasing levels of violence inflicted on the planet and the peril of this violence.

Pinker's conception of moral progress takes no account of the ecological violence and destruction that came with the rise of modernism. He wants us to credit modernism for all our material and physical comforts, and also for giving us access to "the higher and nobler things in life" that could now fit in a tool that could go into pants pockets. But again, what of the unsurpassed ecological violence and destruction that modernism promotes and thrives on? The problem with Pinker's thesis is that modernism subscribes to a narrow conception of violence. No doubt, the world is much better off without slavery, the burning of heretics and witches, and all the other horrible things that Pinker highlights. But Jainism and Buddhism would also have sought to end these abominations thousands of years ago. Moreover, what native and indigenous civilization has made a comparable level of investment in creating, acquiring, and stockpiling weapons of mass destruction that could potentially bring the world to an end within moments?

Pinker's lists, charts, and diagrams are impressive as well as seductive. We do seem to be morally evolving and the world does seem to be approaching an evolutionary landmark. How many of us, after all, are ready to give up all the material and physical comforts that modernity has provided? Who wants to live in a society with different ambitions? In shaping our moral imagination, modernity's definition of progress seems natural to us. It even feels like the only definition of moral progress. Such certainty pervades Pinker's book. He adheres rigidly to one notion of moral progress. He would probably contend that the proof is in the numbers—the rest of the world wants desperately to move to and live in the western/European world where modernism is the status quo. But the ecological destruction and peril that comes with modernism are now pushing us to look anew at modernism's definition of moral progress. For how can moral progress be making for the destruction of our own habitat by our own doing? What does our contamination of all the world's lakes, rivers, and oceans mean for moral progress? Evidently, the world's natural order has no intention of submitting to modernism's view of moral progress. There will be no tolerance of all the ecological violence and destruction. Yet stopping this violence is by no means merely about changing our environmental practices. This ecological violence is at the heart of modernity and the moral progress that modernism promises. Stopping this ecological violence demands nothing less than the ending of modernism. No amount of repurposing, recycling, and reusing will suffice to save modernism.

The world's natural order seems to be challenging us to arrive at a new definition of moral progress. This involves looking anew at what constitutes violence. As Jainism and Buddhism long ago recognized, because everything is related and connected to everything else, violence never happens in a vacuum. There are always consequences and implications that fall back on us. Violence constitutes any action, practice, or arrangement that impedes the flourishing of life, including all life. Jainism and Buddhism recognized long ago that to affirm life is to end violence. As such, the promotion of all life must be foundational to a new worldview that could save us from the ecological peril that is now upon us. This will make for ways of perceiving the world where everything is related and connected. So when we are challenged to account for the violence that comes with forest fires, volcanoes, tsunamis, earthquakes, and tornadoes, we will point to the life-affirming nature of these supposedly destructive forces, showcasing the many ways these forces are vital for ecologies to blossom and flourish.

CHAPTER 20

ON VALUING OBJECTIVITY

THE WESTERN/EUROPEAN WORLD PROFESSES TO value truth, reason, and objectivity. These concepts are born of the belief that our redemption resides outside of us because our bodies are fallible. We have to develop practices and structures that will help us limit and control our passions and emotions, biases and prejudices, instincts and impulses. Supposedly, without being able to exercise dominion over the body, truth, reason, and objectivity will be impossible and chaos will reign. Our redemption is supposedly dependent on us successfully conquering our passions and emotions. Our bodies presumably stand in the way of our progress and prosperity, which also means that our progress and prosperity are defined and measured by our success in conquering our bodies.

Our development of vast hierarchies and bureaucracies is all for the purpose of conquering the body. Theoretically, the goal of every hierarchy and bureaucracy is to promote truth, reason, and objectivity. This is supposedly how order will come into the world. There are also methods, techniques, and thought systems that promise to deliver truth, reason, and objectivity. This is why, for instance, methods courses are integral to science. Supposedly, through the employment of various methodologies and technologies we will achieve the objectivity that is so indispensable for the discovery of truth and the promotion of reason. This is why rigor tends to be synonymous with objectivity. To be rigorous is supposedly to be proficient—that is, to have mastery over various methodologies and technologies. To be rigorous is also to have control over the environment, population, and outcomes that surround our inquiry. This is why research typically begins with a hypothesis—a promise of what will be found and within what parameters. To be rigorous is to be able to control and predict—to do what science promises and progress presumably demands. So the narrative found in curriculums is that the purpose of methods courses is to make us methodologically and technologically proficient, which in turn helps us to push forward the mission of science, and which in turn presumably promotes progress and prosperity by helping us conquer the body. Supposedly, without our various methodologies and technologies, we would have no means to properly conquer the body, and thereby no means of achieving a lasting progress and prosperity. This is also what is so seductive about methods courses—acquiring a power that allows us to control and predict how the world works.

A ruler is a technology. It is meant to help us control and predict. It is also meant to help us attain the objectivity that science values. Two feet in Africa is two feet in Asia, North America, and Australia. All that remains is our proficiency in using a ruler. Any error can only come from our lack of proficiency. But behind the invention of the ruler is the belief that human beings are capable of inventing methods and tools that will allow us to understand the world precisely and objectively—devoid of the intrusion of our emotions and passions, biases and prejudices, impulses and instincts. To understand the world objectively is also supposedly to understand the world fairly. That two feet in Africa is also two feet in Asia allows us to make certain kinds of universal claims and comparisons. The ruler lessens the diversity between Africa and Asia. Now both share a common set of values. But what exactly is a ruler measuring, and what makes this measurement objective? Simply put, what is two feet? It is no different than what is four feet, six feet, and eight feet—an ideological construct. Every method, every technology is an ideological creation. The ruler is capturing and propagating a certain conception of time and space, specifically the conception that it is the civilization that brought the ruler into the world. This conception of time and space is also born of a certain moral imagination. To want to measure the world precisely already assumes that the world can be precisely measured, that doing so is important, and that human beings have the capacity to do so. All of this could possibly be true. But there is nothing objective about what a ruler is doing. Objectivity is an ideological construct, really an ideological illusion. To measure is to impose our own conception of time and space on the world. Yet methods courses make no such admission. Science is only capable of giving us the power to predict and control what science makes controllable and predictable. Our methodologies and technologies only give us the means to observe and measure a world that is already imagined and conceived. This, again, is why science can be in the hypothesis business and promise findings that meet the highest degrees of certainty.

But what of the rest of the world? Can the rest of the world allow a ruler to pass as merely a ruler? That is, can the rest of the world allow methods courses to be merely methods courses, and thereby aid and abet the separation of ideology from methodology? Who profits most from the promotion of this illusory separation, meaning whose interest is best served by the supposed objectivity that science claims to offer? Science would no doubt claim that this objectivity equally serves the interests of all. After all, science is presumably devoid of biases and prejudices. Only the truth supposedly matters. But no ideology equally serves the interests of all as no ideology equally privileges every belief, every norm, every expectation. This is humanly impossible. Ideologies exclude and discriminate because there are only so many things human beings can value and believe. So again, whose interests are best served by the objectivity that science peddles?

Objectivity is by no means an easy notion to knock down. It is at the heart of all that science promises. Also, what would be left of science without the methods that promise to deliver objective results and findings? What would be the value of findings that presumably lack objectivity? Indeed, what would become of the status of science without objectivity? What also would become of our vast hierarchies and bureaucracies without objectivity? To predict and control is about first and foremost controlling our own emotions and passions, biases and prejudices, impulses and instincts from contaminating our results and findings. In this case, objectivity means purity, which is assumed to be a good thing. What then becomes of our impression of the human condition? Left to our own devices, we supposedly pollute and contaminate. We must therefore be hierarchically and bureaucratically controlled. Objectivity also means controlling the persons under study. We want samples and populations that are neatly organized and categorized. We want clean data. We want, for the sake of objectivity, to be able to precisely measure the impact of various variables on various populations. Highly homogenous samples and populations are desired, which means that objectivity requires removing all of the diversity that is naturally found in all populations. But such diversity can never be completely removed. We only have the illusion of doing so.

Science has us believing that our diversity is a problem. It pollutes and contaminates. It impedes the production of objective results and findings. Thus the diversity found in populations must also be controlled. This is what the introduction of methods courses brings to peoples throughout the world when western curriculums are introduced for the sake of promoting progress and prosperity. We come to view our own diversity as a problem that must be controlled in order to produce findings that will ultimately give us the credentials to make policy so that progress and prosperity can be had. So our research begins with us sorting and categorizing our populations into variables to be statistically analyzed to produce objective findings. We sort by age, occupation, gender, religion, race, and a few other boxes that are relatively standard. We then apply the treatment and look at the effects of the treatment on these variables. We then report the measured effects and why these results are reliable and generalizable. Integral to all of this is our belief that our diversity can be controlled and be reduced to a set of variables. We simply assume that the variables that matter to us also matter to the population, and even equally so? In most cases, the population has no involvement in the shaping of our research, such as sharing with us which variables and issues matter. Controlling the diversity of our populations usually means keeping our subjects silenced. Rigorous research demands that our subjects—again, subjects—must comply obediently with our instructions and perform all assigned tasks dutifully. Neither does the population under study have any involvement in how the data will be analyzed and synthesized. All of this silencing is presumably what objectivity demands. It also requires our complicity. However, no amount of boxes can adequately command and represent our diversity. Every variable is related to every other variable in all manner of ways. Also, the number of variables that could be derived from any population is simply endless. It is impossible to analyze the relationships between all these variables. Moreover, statistically significant relationships will always arise when sample sizes are large and variables are many. But again, the subjects will usually have no involvement in determining what relationships are important. We will make that decision, as we supposedly possess the expertise to know what is best.

Controlling and lessening a population's diversity also means controlling and lessening that population's ambiguity, complexity, and humanity. This is how human beings become research subjects—subjects to be passively probed, analyzed, and hypothesized. We in turn are dehumanized by the process. The kind of control that objectivity requires of us dehumanizes us by demanding the stripping away of our own diversity, complexity, ambiguity, and humanity. For what becomes of the human experience without our emotions and passions, instincts and impulses, even our biases and prejudices? How did objectivity come to deserve this kind of price, and what is the pursuit of this illusory objectivity doing to us? We become what we do. To treat others as objects is to become an object. To make others voiceless is to make ourselves voiceless. The negation of our humanity can be found in sentences that read, "This study investigates the effects of…" or "This study concludes…" It is human beings who investigate, who conclude. But this kind of human displacement is what objectivity demands. It must be the study that investigates and concludes. There can be no mention of the emotions and passions that bring us to the study, including our own confusions and frustrations, turmoil and despair.

CHAPTER 21

ON THE RISE OF CIVILIZATIONS

NIALL FERGUSON, LAURENCE A. TISCH Professor of History at Harvard University, contends that "the rise of Western civilization is the single most important historical phenomenon of the second half of the second millennium after Christ" (2011, p. 8). In *Civilization: The West And The Rest*, Ferguson takes on the "challenge" of explaining how this ascendancy occurred. "What was it about the civilization of Western Europe after the fifteenth century that allowed it to trump the outwardly superior empires of the Orient?" (p. 8). He credits "six identifiable novel complexes of institutions and associated ideas and behaviors." These are (with brief definitions provided by Ferguson):

1. Competition—"a decentralization of both political and economic life, which created the launch-pad for both nation-states and capitalism."
2. Science—"a way of studying, understanding and ultimately changing the natural world, which gave the West (among other things) a major military advantage over the Rest."
3. Property rights—"the rule of law as a means of protecting private owners and peacefully resolving disputes between them, which formed the basis for the most stable form of representative government."
4. Medicine—"a branch of science that allowed a major improvement in health and life expectancy, beginning in Western societies, but also in their colonies."

5. The Consumer Society—"a mode of material living in which the production and purchase of clothing and other consumer goods play a central economic role, and without which the Industrial Revolution would have been unsustainable."
6. The Work Ethic—"a moral framework and mode of activity derivable from (among other sources) Protestant Christianity, which provided the glue for the dynamic and potentially unstable society created by 1 to 5" (p. 13).

But Ferguson is aspiring to do much more than merely account for the ascendancy of Western civilization. He is implicitly trying to account for the supposed unsurpassed superiority of Western civilization. What makes this civilization superior to all others? Or, why do other civilizations remain determined to adopt the ways and institutions of this civilization? Presumably, only by coming to terms with this supposed superiority can we begin to understand what the decline of Western civilization means for the world, the forces, practices, and institutions aiding and abetting this decline, and what we can do to impede and even reverse this decline.

Ferguson believes that only horrible things will come with the decline and fall of Western civilization. He uses the Roman Empire ("the first version of the West") as a case study to warn against how "a startlingly sophisticated system" where "scholarship flourished" and also where there was law, medicine, shopping malls, sophisticated infrastructural systems like aqueducts, and an abundance of food, could decline dramatically, "undone by barbarian invasions and internal divisions." Ferguson wants us to stop this decline and fall from happening again.

Every civilization is born of a certain imagination. To believe is to imagine, and what we believe shapes what we imagine. Eventually we create the world we imagine, which in turn reinforces what we believe. The only world we are capable of creating and even understanding is the one we are capable of imagining. What we imagine the world to be reveals what we believe is possible and also morally tolerable and permissible. So at the heart of every civilization is a human limitation—human beings are only capable of imagining and believing so much. What this means, amongst many other things, is that no civilization can ever claim to reflect the limits of human potentiality. No doubt, certain civilizations are morally superior to others. But even the unsurpassed ascendancy of a civilization can do nothing to disconnect us from the limits of our imagination. This is the primary problem with Ferguson's thesis. He shows no appreciation of the relationship between ontology and epistemology, imagination and civilization.

Ferguson wants us to assume that the ascendancy of Western civilization affirms a superiority that can neither be matched nor surpassed. Indeed, the rest of the world does seem determined to become Westernized. But why should the imagination that drives Western civilization be the limits of our own imagination, and ultimately the worlds we are capable of realizing? What do we gain by impeding ourselves this way? For instance, what about the imagination of the slaves that were victimized and brutalized by that "startlingly sophisticated system" that was the Roman Empire? Why should these slaves have no right to imagine a new civilization? In the end, what must we do to emancipate our imagination so as to create a more humane and less cruel and violent world? What environs and resources do we need?

CHAPTER 22

On The Nature of Institutions

We generally assume that the success of a civilization can be determined by the integrity and character of its institutions. Presumably, good institutions make for great civilizations as much as great civilizations make for good institutions. Political scientists and policymakers are always stressing to Third World nations the importance of creating good institutions by promoting accountability, transparency, and all else that would impede corruption and incompetence. Supposedly, through the creation of good institutions developing nations would achieve the kind of progress and prosperity that is supposedly found in developed nations. The importance of institutions in our narrative of progress and prosperity can be seen in the enormous amount of academic resources that we devote to studying and theorizing about institutions, and credentialing persons with all kinds of degrees that supposedly reflect expertise and knowledge in managing institutions. Indeed, career advancement is difficult without one of these credentials. Just as well, with institutions being assumed to be vital for the progress and prosperity of developing nations, the governments of these nations have also made enormous investments in equipping locals with these credentials. This is supposedly how developing nations will achieve progress and prosperity—by equipping their people with the expertise and knowledge to make their institutions efficient.

Integral to the success of institutions, according to Hugh Heclo (2008), Clarence J. Robinson Professor of Public Affairs at George Mason University, and prior to that Professor of Government at Harvard University, is learning to think institutionally. In *On Thinking Institutionally*, Heclo writes, "Institutional failure, and the distrust it engenders, is the result of people continually failing to live up to legitimate expectations attached to their positions of responsibility" (p. 25). Heclo claims that this failure is always looming, as human beings are inherently imperfect. The purpose of institutions is to help us "rise above" our imperfect human nature. Specifically, "we turn to institutions and their standards to help restrain and channel our ordinary human impulses to lie, cheat, and steal (among other numerous faults that come naturally to our species)" (p. 25). In short, Heclo believes that without institutions, chaos and debauchery will reign and progress and prosperity will be impossible. He claims that "Thinking institutionally means being mindful of one's duty. And that means accepting that there are anguishing choices to be made in matters of personal duty and organizational loyalty" (p. 91). However, Heclo also claims that when "institutions fail, it is mainly a matter of people failing institutions. People fail institutions by failing to think and act with due regard to the valued purposes embodied in institutions" (pp. 126-127). This failure, according Heclo, "does not consist in simply making mistakes, errors, and miscalculations. It consists in failures of being" (p. 127).

But what Heclo misses is that institutions also require us to believe certain things in order to make that kind of being possible. We must, first and foremost, be willing to believe that chaos and debauchery will reign without institutions. Heclo would no doubt claim that this is simply about recognizing a fact rather than forming a belief. But history only gives us the impression that this is a fact. We can compellingly argue that chaos and debauchery have origins in our failure to act relationally, communally, or even ecologically. But first let us look at the case study that Heclo uses to showcase people thinking institutionally—the people involved in creating and ratifying the United States Constitution. Heclo believes that the founding of the United States would have been impossible without the founding fathers thinking institutionally, as in believing that creating a nation that was, to use Madison's words, "the last hope of true liberty on the face of the Earth," was more important than the pursuit of shortsighted partisan goals. But what did all of this exemplary institutional thinking by Madison, Jefferson, Adams, and company do for the emancipation of those held in servitude and bondage? That is, how did serving the value and purpose of liberty by these men come to do nothing for the liberty of slaves? Heclo claims that thinking institutionally is about embodying a certain set of noble values that protect an institution's integrity and prosperity. It is foremost about recognizing our obligation to the institution rather than our own professional advancement. This, again, is why Heclo characterizes thinking institutionally as a way of being. It is presumably a morally superior kind of being.

Heclo's point is that institutions save us from ourselves and also make us better human beings. Good institutions encourage us to think institutionally, which in turn presumably makes us better human beings by cultivating in us noble pursuits. However, as slaves had no voluntary participation in any institution, and no rewards for thinking institutionally, what explains the ability of most slaves to sustain such a rich and deep humanity in the face of so much brutality and depravity from those who Heclo celebrates for thinking institutionally? Without access to good institutions, how did slaves come to be morally superior to those who professed to value liberty? Where is the relationship here between moral development and thinking institutionally?

We can become fully human relationally, communally, ecologically, and communicationally. There is no one way to become so. But the reality of over 350 years of slavery and Jim Crow reveals that institutions diminish our understanding of moral development. Moral development evidently involves much more than thinking institutionally. Ultimately, moral development involves courage, as in the courage to love, to forgive, to share, to empathize, to imagine, to believe, as well as the courage to defy the normalizing and conforming pressures that make institutions possible. By promoting various normalizing and conforming pressures, institutions block our moral development by impeding our ability to act courageously. Institutions and moral development are in conflict with each other. This is how Madison, Jefferson, Adams, and company were able to advocate for liberty and also keep other human beings in servitude and bondage. Thinking institutionally is about thinking institutionally. Moral development, on the other hand, involves pushing against our limits, and challenging the legitimacy of the limits imposed on us by others. In this regard, moral development involves challenging all the status quo values. The progress and prosperity that will come from the promotion of institutions will be different from that which will come from the promotion of moral development. Institutions will only give us the impression of moral development. In fact, institutions give us a shallow view of progress and prosperity, one that emphasizes efficiency, productivity, and functionality.

A review of the manuals that developing nations are using to guide public policy reveals the belief that cultivating good institutions is necessary for progress and prosperity, and that the focus should be on equipping locals with expertise to manage institutions effectively. But there are much more expansive and constructive ways to look at progress and prosperity. We can do so relationally, communally, ecologically, and communicationally. All of these emergent perspectives make plain to us that our own well-being is bound up with the well-being of others and with the condition of the planet. We will be challenged to arrive at new definitions of progress and prosperity that are in harmony with this axiom or self-evident truth. All of this is important for at least saving ourselves from the ecological peril that now looms. Then again, most likely these alternative definitions will never be pursued until history makes change inevitable.

Thinking institutionally is presumably about thinking in terms of what is best for the institution. But why should this be our foremost concern? How do we know that what is best for the institution is ultimately best for us? Heclo never broaches these kinds of questions. We are merely told that "Thinking institutionally means being mindful of one's duty. And that means accepting that there are anguishing choices to be made in matters of personal duty and organizational loyalty" (p. 91). Translation, thinking institutionally can mean anything. How one person thinks institutionally can be fundamentally different from how another thinks institutionally, making for conflicting outcomes. This can be vividly seen in the civil rights movement.

Many in the civil rights movement believed that unjust laws should be publicly violated. However, many White liberals believed that doing so would set a dangerous precedent, ultimately undermining the integrity of the justice system. Civil rights leaders were advised by these liberals to use the courts, local and state legislatures, Congress, and the White House to change and remove these laws. Doing so would ensure that the integrity of these institutions remain intact and eventually be available to the first Black president. In fact, many openly criticized the civil rights movement for refusing to be patient, and by that, failing to think institutionally. In this case, this meant putting the interest and well-being of one's country over one's race.

A case in point would be Martin Luther King's "Letter from Birmingham [Alabama] Jail." King was being chastised for taking an unpopular position—demanding that the United States' apartheid system be immediately dismantled. The popular view, as seen by the position of the Christian theologians who opposed King, was for African Americans to be patient and remain law-abiding. For these theologians, King was the culprit. He was the one causing mischief and inviting chaos by encouraging African Americans to disobey various segregation laws. Indeed, what is striking about the Birmingham case is that King was going up against theologians, those who were supposed to know well that the cause of justice could involve neither patience nor tolerance. There was nothing that King was doing that was contrary to the teachings of Jesus Christ. He was merely siding unequivocally and unconditionally with whom Jesus Christ refers to as "the least of these."

Martin Luther King, Jr. was doing what Jesus Christ said Christians must do, exercise moral courage—stand courageously, unequivocally, and nonviolently for the betterment of all peoples, which includes refusing to obey unjust laws. In fact, according to King, "there is nothing new about this kind of civil disobedience. It was evidenced sublimely in the refusal of Shadrach, Meshach and Abednego to obey the laws of Nebuchadnezzar, on the ground that a higher moral law was at stake. It was practiced superbly by the early Christians, who were willing to face hungry lions and the excruciating pain of chopping blocks rather than submit to certain unjust laws of the Roman Empire." As to how to distinguish a just law from an unjust law, King said:

One may well ask: "How can you advocate breaking some laws and obeying others?" The answer lies in the fact that there are two types of laws: just and unjust. I would be the first to advocate obeying just laws. One has not only a legal but a moral responsibility to obey just laws. Conversely, one has a moral responsibility to disobey unjust laws. I would agree with St. Augustine that "an unjust law is no law at all." Now, what is the difference between the two? How does one determine whether a law is just or unjust? A just law is a man made code that squares with the moral law or the law of God. An unjust law is a code that is out of harmony with the moral law. To put it in the terms of St. Thomas Aquinas: An unjust law is a human law that is not rooted in eternal law and natural law. Any law that uplifts human personality is just. Any law that degrades human personality is unjust. All segregation statutes are unjust because segregation distorts the soul and damages the personality. It gives the segregator a false sense of superiority and the segregated a false sense of inferiority. Segregation, to use the terminology of the Jewish philosopher Martin Buber, substitutes an "I it" relationship for an "I thou" relationship and ends up relegating persons to the status of things. Hence segregation is not only politically, economically and sociologically unsound, it is morally wrong and sinful. Paul Tillich has said that sin is separation. Is not segregation an existential expression of man's tragic separation, his awful estrangement, his terrible sinfulness? Thus it is that I can urge men to obey the 1954 decision of the Supreme Court, for it is morally right; and I can urge them to disobey segregation ordinances, for they are morally wrong.

King, of course, was in no way encouraging chaos and depravity. For King, "One who breaks an unjust law must do so openly, lovingly, and with a willingness to accept the penalty. I submit that an individual who breaks a law that conscience tells him is unjust, and who willingly accepts the penalty of imprisonment in order to arouse the conscience of the community over its injustice, is in reality expressing the highest respect for law." King was merely assuming that human beings are capable of acting reflectively and mindfully, and that doing so is necessary for moral development and the flourishing of justice.

But who is now ready to argue and criticize Martin Luther King for refusing to be patient? What about Nat Turner and John Brown? Were both also guilty of failing to think institutionally? What about Harriett Tubman? What did encouraging slaves to run away do for the legal sanctity of property rights? Still, Heclo refers to slavery as a "hard" case as regards thinking institutionally. He challenges us to recognize that there was a "Southern ideology" that had "a morally grounded outlook" based on "the conviction that the institution of slavery, when rightly managed, was ordained by God" (p. 155). After all, "God's chosen people, the Jews, had been a slaveholding people and suffered no divine reprimand for being so" (p. 155). Heclo claims "Only if we are willing to enter into their admittedly foreign framework of institutional thinking can we hear what at least some well-intentioned Southerners concerned for human welfare were trying to say" (p. 155). However, this generous description of those persons who held other human beings in bondage and servitude borders on the surreal. But such is the order of thinking institutionally. We must look at the world from the perspective of the institutions, as our prosperity is supposedly dependent on institutions saving us from chaos and debauchery. This is what White liberals and many theologians were demanding of Martin Luther King, Jr.—be mindful of what will supposedly become of us without our institutions remaining intact. Chaos and debauchery will presumably reign. These liberals and theologians wanted the civil rights movement to look at what was supposedly the larger picture, just as how Heclo is now telling us to do with Southern Whites. We are presumably obligated to do everything to avoid chaos and debauchery. This is our prime directive. Nearly anything that we do in the name of this directive can possibly be seen as morally tolerable. This is what Nat Turner, John Brown, and Martin Luther King, Jr., were up against. Thinking institutionally is about favoring order. Order can never be jeopardized.

But for Nat Turner, John Brown, Martin Luther King, Jr., and company, order was the problem. Order means status quo and legitimacy and truth.

Order was making impossible the emancipation of African Americans. For emancipation to happen, chaos had to be embraced and encouraged. Anything less than a full embrace of chaos makes for a reactionary politics, one that mistakes inclusion for emancipation, progress for revolution. Embracing chaos gives us moral clarity by reminding us of our mortality. It also releases of the fears, anxieties, and paranoia that impede our acting boldly and courageously. This failure to fully embrace chaos eventually corroded and trivialized the civil rights movement, reducing it to merely a struggle for inclusion rather than revolution. This was most apparent when nearly every civil rights organization publicly condemned Martin Luther King, Jr., for openly opposing the Vietnam War.

We generally want persons to be honest, competent, and noble. But how do we achieve this kind of being? Organizational theorists would generally contend that the answer involves developing and upholding organizational/institutional structures that would instill the desired behaviors and outcomes. Good institutions have norms, rituals, and traditions that cultivate the behaviors and practices that make for good institutions. This belief pervades discussions of democracy. We hear in various reports that democracy is new to many of these developing nations. We hear that developing these new institutions is going to take time. There are going to be setbacks and stumbles. We are advised to be patient. We are told that eventually these institutions will mature and take hold. But what did the supposed maturity of the institution of democracy do for African Americans for nearly 350 years? What also did the courts, Congress, local and state legislatures, and the White House do over this period for African American that is worthy of praise?

Who would now claim that after nearly 400 years all these institutions are functioning effectively, efficiently, and nobly? Also, what is the case to be made that these institutions are responsible for our moral evolution, such as ending slavery and Jim Crow? What would have been the prospects of Congress ending Jim Crow without the civil rights movement taking to the streets? Would women have achieved the right to vote without agitating, protesting, and organizing?

History undermines most arguments favoring institutions, including the claim that institutions can make us efficient and competent. In fact, emergent perspectives in organizational theory, as found in books with titles like *Liberation Management*, now advise organizations to become less and less institutional and hierarchical. Organizations are advised to shift responsibility and accountability away from institutions to human beings. We function best when we are directly and singularly responsible for our own actions, decisions, and lack thereof. Emergent perspectives in organizational theory, as found in books with titles like *Chaos Management*, also now advise organizations to embrace and even nurture chaos. We are told that order is illusory and also impedes the kind of struggling with ambiguity that is necessary for becoming human and promoting innovation. In short, emergent perspectives in organizational theory view institutions as a threat to human development. We are advised against trying to build institutions that could presumably improve our control and command of human beings. What is increasingly different is our view of the human condition. Instead of viewing human beings as inherently imperfect, emergent perspectives in organizational theory view us in terms of capacity and potentiality. The focus is on identifying the processes and practices that could make our capacities and potentialities flourish. Besides making us—rather than our institutions—efficient and competent, the goal is to make us resilient and comfortable with diversity and disruption. That is, the goal is first and foremost to create a better human being rather than to make a better institution. Better human beings will eventually make for systems that are just, decent, and equitable.

CHAPTER 23

ON HUMAN RIGHTS

In *Human Rights As Politics And Idolatry*, Michael Ignatieff, Director of the Carr Center for Human Rights Policy at Harvard University, sets out to make a definitive case for human rights. He adopts a minimalist approach that is based on negative freedom—human rights are about protecting all human beings from abuse and cruelty. "The doctrine of human rights," Ignatieff (2001) writes, "is morally universal because it says that all human beings need certain specific freedoms "from"; it does not go on to define what their freedom "to" should consist in. In this sense, it is a less prescriptive universalism than the world's religions: it articulates standards of human decency without violating rights of cultural autonomy" (p. 75). Ignatieff claims that human rights require no belief that there is anything "sacred about human beings" or that human beings are "entitled to worship or ultimate respect" (p. 83). Neither is there any reason to have a morally elevated view of human beings in order to justify all human beings being entitled to human rights protections. For Ignatieff, the case for human rights "is that they are necessary to protect individuals from violence and abuse, and if it is asked why, the only possible answer is historical. Human rights is the language through which individuals have created a defense of their autonomy against the oppression of religion, state, family, and group" (p. 83).

The primary function of human rights is to protect individual autonomy, which in turn is assumed to be necessary for social and economic security and prosperity. According to Ignatieff, "Without the freedom to articulate and express political opinions, without freedom of speech and assembly, together with freedom of property rights, agents cannot organize themselves to struggle for social and economic security" (p. 90). Human rights also assume moral reciprocity—human beings have the ability to imagine the pain being inflicted on others and would prefer to be spared that pain themselves. Avoid doing to others as you prefer others avoid doing to you. Ignatieff writes, "Such facts about human beings—that they feel pain, that they are free to do good and abstain from evil—provide the basis by which we believe that all human beings should be protected from cruelty" (p. 89).

What Michael Ignatieff is trying to do in *Human Rights As Politics and Idolatry* is laudable. In a world that has seen so much cruelty, any initiative to end or even lessen cruelty should be encouraged. The model that Ignatieff lays out, which is found in the Universal Declaration of Human Rights that was first adopted by the United Nations in 1948, seems reasonable and certainly minimalist. All that is being demanded is that cultures and nations refrain from cruelty and abuse. How difficult is this proposition? Why would any society want to be named as supporting abuse and cruelty? But herein is where Ignatieff's human rights approach begins to encounter problems. What is considered cruelty is shaped by cultural, political, and historical forces. In many cultures, female genital mutilation would never be defined as cruelty. Neither would the death penalty, nor the sentencing of juveniles to sentences without the possibility of parole, nor the incarceration of persons for non-violent offenses, be seen as cruel in other cultures. What also of situational forces, as when a nation believes that torture is necessary to protect the interests and well-being of the common good? Moreover, according to Ignatieff, the case against cruelty begins on the recognition of moral reciprocity—our being able to imagine the pain others are experiencing and our desire to be spared that pain. But what of a society that still believes that pain is good and persons should be subject to pain (punishment) for doing wrong?

Ignatieff claims that a human rights approach offers "a less prescriptive universalism than the world's religions" by articulating "standards of human decency without violating rights of cultural autonomy" (p. 75). But whose standards of human decency? Yes, rape and genocide are universally abominable. But history and ideology play a significant role in shaping our definitions and standards of human decency, and this will always be the case. Ignatieff contends that when differences occur, deliberation should be encouraged. However, in the end, the rest of the world must be ready to use military force to ensure all peoples have the protections of these predetermined standards of decency. This brings us back to the subject of pain and it being a necessary evil. For what is the purpose of military force? How could military force be effective, in this case as serving the supposed common good of human rights, without inflicting pain?

Then there is the matter of autonomy. Ignatieff claims that a human rights approach is necessary to achieve autonomy, and that autonomy is necessary for social and economic security. So autonomy is important. It is impeded by the threat of cruelty and abuse. But are these the only threats to autonomy, or even the greatest threats to autonomy? Moreover, is all autonomy morally equal? What about the ideological, institutional, and epistemological structures that limit our moral imagination? Instead of being afraid of being abused and tortured, which any person should rightfully fear, what about being afraid of the world's ambiguity? What kind of autonomy can come from persons who are laden with fear and anxiety? How could such persons act boldly and courageously? Ignatieff assumes that, outside of the threat of abuse and torture, autonomy is all good. But this view assumes that autonomy is morally equal and should be equally protected. In short, a human rights approach in no way challenges us to look critically at how our ideological, institutional, and epistemological forces limit autonomy by limiting and even impoverishing our moral imagination. Autonomy inherently poses no threat to the status quo. We can still have autonomy and be afraid to act boldly. In that case, what is the value of autonomy? Again, according to Ignatieff, autonomy is important for social and economic security. Historically, this is no doubt true. A society with even a semblance of autonomy will always be better than one without any. But because autonomy is morally unequal, what constitutes social and economic security can be fundamentally different and even conflicting. For instance, what about those nations that profess to value autonomy, and also value and promote social and economic systems that make for ecological peril? What is the value of any autonomy that is responsible for creating and sustaining these kinds of life-negating systems? What about the right to be spared the deadly fallout that comes from the autonomy that drives these systems? How is this right any less important than other kinds of human rights?

All of this returns us to the minimalist view that Ignatieff uses to frame the human rights perspective. Ignatieff claims that a universal conception of decency can only be achieved by a minimalist approach—asking for barely the minimum, in this case asking groups to only refrain from being cruel. To do differently presumably violates cultural autonomy and threatens the world's cultural diversity. However, besides being ideologically impossible, Ignatieff's human rights approach is also ecologically impossible. It is contrary to the laws and rhythms that govern life. Ecologies achieve harmony with other ecologies by becoming increasingly dependent on each other. This ecological dependency cultivates ecological diversity and ecological resiliency. Ecological diversity would be impossible without ecological dependency. In this case diversity binds rather than fragments. From an ecological perspective, cultural autonomy is death. So also is any approach that impedes the rise of ecological dependency. We know well that cultures and civilizations thrive by drawing abundantly upon the resources, talents, and influences of other cultures and civilizations. Thus why should that kind of borrowing, cross-pollinating, and intertwining be discouraged now for the sake of protecting cultural autonomy? Access to other cultures and civilizations enriches our autonomy. Autonomy is ecological. How much access we have to other ecologies will shape how we exercise autonomy. As such, being committed to the growth and promotion of autonomy obligates us to be concerned with what is happening with other ecologies and our ability to draw upon the resources, talents, and influences that those ecologies offer.

How do we achieve a world that is devoid of cruelty? An ecological approach would advise that we do the opposite to what Ignatieff advises. We promote ecological integration and dependency. We should strive to organically rather than imperially dismantle and undermine the forces and structures that block ecological integration, collaboration, and cooperation. We can name this an *obligations approach* as the focus is on identifying and expanding our ecological obligations to others. But what exactly are these obligations? How can we organically promote these obligations? How can we embody these obligations? An obligations approach gets us beyond the many problems that surround the human rights approach. It unilaterally imposes no standards of human decency. Instead, an obligations approach takes an emergent view. Universal standards of decency will emerge through the promotion of integration, collaboration, and cooperation. Eventually different ecologies will achieve a degree of harmony and equilibrium that allows for the most diversity, resiliency, and stability. Also, an obligations approach gives us a better understanding of the minority problem that deeply and rightfully concerns Ignatieff.

Human rights are fundamentally about protecting minority groups from cruelty. They give the rest of the world moral permission to intervene and protect minority groups from persecution and even extermination. Presumably, without human rights, the rest of the world has no moral permission to defend any kind of intervention. But an obligations approach also gives us moral permission to defend minority groups from cruelty. An ecology thrives by cultivating diversity and equity. To conspire to impede diversity, such as persecuting minority groups, ultimately undermines the flourishing of an ecology and all the species that constitute that ecology. Also, the well-being of an ecology can be reliably determined by examining the prosperity of the most vulnerable species in that ecology. An ecology thrives only when the most vulnerable species that share that ecology also thrive. An obligations approach would focus on exposing the tensions and conflicts that majority groups suppress in order to coalesce power and privilege. Minority groups are nothing but political constructions. These constructions are for the sake of allocating and legitimizing power. That a person is defined as a minority merely means that others have the power to influence how that person is defined and experienced. It is much more than simply deciding what box a person will check. It is about the fact that the person still has to check a box.

But there is also power in refusing to check a box and defining ourselves on our own terms. The oppressed, marginalized, and forsaken are never without power. Of course, the power is never comparable to what others possess.

But there is still power to affirm, to resist, to contest—that is, the power to remain human in the face of evil. An obligations approach emphasizes the harnessing of this power. We are first and foremost obligated to remain human in the face of evil. Emancipation without dignity is nothing. We merely become the new perpetrators of cruelty. An obligations approach saves us from this fate. We are obligated to treat those who abuse and torture us humanely and compassionately for the sake of our never becoming abusive and cruel and allowing these evils to live on in the world. This is what a human rights approach misses by focusing on the rights of individuals. It assumes that the condition of my humanity has no bearing on the humanity of others. Presumably, only my rights matter, and I can presumably use any means to protect these rights. But this view of the human condition, which even psychology is now beginning to recognize, is false. The condition of our own humanity is bound up with the humanity of others as well as with the condition of the world. Our fates are intertwined, which means that our obligations to each other cannot be separated or suppressed. In order to rid the world of abuse and cruelty, rather than merely protect my minimal human rights, I am obligated to treat even my abuser and torturer humanely and compassionately. This obligation exceeds any human rights I may have, as human rights mean nothing in a world laden with abuse and cruelty. This is how an obligations approach challenges us to look at the world in new ways that fundamentally expand our obligation to each other, and in so doing inherently poses a serious threat to the status quo and the order of things.

Ignatieff believes that there is no need to assume that human beings are sacred beings in order to legitimize human rights. In fact, Ignatieff believes that the human rights approach is attractive because nothing is assumed sacred about human beings. Its appeal resides in its practicality. No human being, regardless of race, creed, or religion, wants to be abused and tortured. But if there is nothing spiritual about human beings, there is certainly much about us that is ecological. This makes the distinction between the human rights approach and the obligations approach significant. The human rights approach puts the focus on the individual. Human rights are individual rights. Human rights protect individual rights. But in the obligations approach, the focus is on the ecology, meaning that the focus is on life. In the human rights approach, the focus is on protecting the individual. We are only committed to protecting the individual from abuse and cruelty. In the human rights approach, human beings only need rights. Save us from abuse and cruelty and all will supposedly be well. Indeed, the human rights approach assumes that the cruelty we inflict upon others has no bearing on us because the condition of our own humanity presumably has no relation to the condition of others' humanity. Protecting our own rights suffices to make for the beginnings of the good life. It is where our obligation to each other presumably begins and ends. But in an obligations approach, because everything is assumed to be related to everything else, what is best for us must also be best for everything else. Our well-being is bound up with the world's well-being because we are bound up with the world as much as the world is bound up with us. There is no place for any practice or arrangement that would divide and separate us from the world and each other.

An obligations approach pushes us to look anew at our role and place in the world. It assumes that the origins of cruelty can be found in our division and separation. In the human rights approach, cruelty is the problem. However, in the obligations approach, cruelty is merely an expression of the problem. The problem is our separation from the world and each other, or our illusory separation from the world and each other. End this separation and cruelty will disappear from the world. So whereas the human rights approach would have us focus on ending cruelty, an obligations approach would have focus on ending separation by promoting union, collaboration, and integration. Besides giving us a different way of thinking about what threatens the world, an obligations approach gives us a different way of imagining what the world could be and our role in making those worlds possible.

CHAPTER 24

On Democracy and Government

THERE IS A GROWING POLITICAL constituency, often referred to as the natural rights movement, which believes that democracy is a morally and politically bankrupt system. It is nothing, according to this movement, but a pretext that governments use to limit our liberty and autonomy. That is, rather than an instrument of liberty, government, under the pretext of safeguarding democracy, limits our liberty by enacting laws that diminish our exercising of full control over our lives. It also impedes liberty by coercively taking away resources from persons who fairly earned those resources through discipline and diligence. The natural rights movement contends that government then uses those resources to foster dependency.

The natural rights movement also claims that government's redistribution of other people's wealth encourages moral depravity by taking away incentives for many other persons to act responsibly, beginning with being responsible for one's well-being and prosperity. This moral depravity in turn further legitimizes government as it takes on the responsibility of protecting us from this moral degeneracy. The natural rights movement claims that government eventually takes advantage of our dependency and becomes abusive, taking more and more of our resources and denying us less and less liberty. Government expansion comes at the cost of liberty. For proponents of the natural rights movement, liberty means being responsible for one's own well-being and prosperity. Without being held responsible for our own well-being and prosperity, the expansion of government means an increase in human depravity and also increasing demands for resources—through taxation—to protect us from this depravity. For the natural rights movement, government is a self-perpetuating, self-legitimizing parasite—using taxation to encourage moral depravity under the pretext of promoting democracy and equality. Thus the only way to end this moral depravity is by ending government, which involves recognizing that government is a morally and politically bankrupt system.

Proponents of the natural rights movement claim that democracy violates the world's natural order, such as there being a natural aristocracy amongst human beings. Presumably, redistributing wealth corrupts this natural aristocracy by encouraging the wrong peoples to breed.

> *In the U.S., less than a century of full-blown democracy has resulted in steadily increasing moral degeneration, family and social disintegration, and cultural decay in the form of continually rising rates of divorce, illegitimacy, abortion, and crime. As a result of an ever expanding list of non-discrimination - "affirmative action" - laws and non-discriminatory - multicultural-egalitarian - immigration policies, every nook and cranny of American society is affected by forced integration, and accordingly, social strife and racial, ethnic, and moral-cultural tension and hostility have increased dramatically.* (Hoppe, 2001, p. xiii)

> *It is not government (monarchical or democratic) that is the source of human civilization and social peace but private property, and the recognition and defense of private property rights, contractualism, and individual responsibility.* (Hoppe, 2001, p. 43)

> *But at the same time, and still more importantly, a positive alternative to monarchy and democracy—the idea of a natural order—must be delineated and understood. On the one hand, this involves the recognition that it is not exploitation, either monarchical or democratic, but private property, production, and voluntary exchange that are the ultimate sources of human*

civilization. On the other hand, it involves the recognition of a fundamental sociological insight (which incidentally also helps identify precisely where the historic opposition to monarchy went wrong): that the maintenance and preservation of a private property based exchange economy requires as its sociological presupposition the existence of a voluntarily acknowledged natural elite-a nobilitas naturalis.

The natural outcome of the voluntary transactions between various private property owners is decidedly nonegalitarian, hierarchical, and elitist. As the result of widely diverse human talents, in every society of any degree of complexity a few individuals quickly acquire the status of an elite. Owing to superior achievements of wealth, wisdom, bravery or a combination thereof, some individuals come to possess "natural authority," and their opinions and judgments enjoy widespread respect. Moreover, because of selective mating and marriage and the laws of civil and genetic inheritance, positions of natural authority are more likely than not passed on within a few noble families. It is to the heads of these families with long-established records of superior achievement, farsightedness, and exemplary personal conduct that men turn with their conflicts and complaints against each other, and it is these very leaders of the natural elite who typically act as judges and peacemakers, often free of charge, out of a sense of obligation required and expected of a person of authority or even out of a principled concern for civil justice, as a privately produced "public good." (Hoppe, 2001, p. 71)

All redistribution, regardless of the criterion on which it is based, involves 'taking' from the original owners and/or producers (the 'havers' of something) and 'giving' to non-owners and non-producers (the 'non-havers' of something). The incentive to be an original owner or producer of the thing in question is reduced, and the incentive to be a non-owner and non-producer is raised. Accordingly, as a result of subsidizing individuals because they are poor, there will be more poverty. In subsidizing people because they are unemployed, more unemployment will be created. Supporting single mothers out of tax funds will lead to an increase in single motherhood, 'illegitimacy', and divorce. In outlawing child labor, income is transferred from families with children to childless persons (as a result of the legal restriction on the supply of labor, wage rates will rise). Accordingly, the birthrate will fall. On the other hand, by subsidizing the education of children, the opposite effect is created. Income is transferred from the childless and those with few children to those with many children. As a result the birthrate will increase. (Hoppe, 2001, p. 98)

What follows from all of this? Clearly, Western civilization has been on a course of self-destruction for quite some time. Can this course be stopped, and if so, how? I wish I could be optimistic, but I am not sure that there is sufficient reason for optimism. To be sure, history is ultimately determined by ideas, and ideas can, at least in principle, change almost instantly. But in order for ideas to change it is not sufficient for people to see that something is wrong. At least a significant number must also be intelligent enough to recognize what it is that is wrong. That is, they must understand the basic principles upon which society—human cooperation—rests . . . . And they must have sufficient will power to act accordingly to this insight. But it is precisely this which one must increasingly doubt. Civilization and culture do have a genetic (biological) basis. However, as the result of statism—of forced integration, egalitarianism, welfare policies, and family destruction—the genetic quality of the population has most certainly declined. Indeed, how could it not when success is systematically punished and failure rewarded? Whether intended or not, the welfare state promotes the proliferation of intellectually and morally inferior people and the results would be even worse were it not for the fact that crime rates are particularly high among these people, and that they tend to eliminate each other more frequently. (Hoppe, 2001, pp. 184-185)

The natural rights movement believes that democracy impedes the natural evolution of this supposed natural aristocracy by disingenuously promoting equality and equal rights. Proponents of this movement claim that this natural aristocracy is necessary for stability and prosperity, and point to the fact that the Founding Fathers also believed in preserving this natural aristocracy. Proponents also claim that democracy creates a mob mentality by giving too much power to the majority, especially a narrow majority. Yes, a democracy will allow certain minority groups certain exemptions, but this is the exception rather than the rule. In the end, according to proponents of this natural rights movement, a democracy forces a minority to submit to the will of a majority, regardless of whether the position of the majority is morally sound or otherwise. There is simply nothing in a democracy that obligates a majority to act morally, such as never encroaching on our liberty and autonomy. For proponents of the natural rights movement, liberty is bound up with property rights—being able to act freely on our property. Property is presumably an extension of our person. We can only act freely by having the space that allows us to act so. This is presumably what property rights give us—our own space to act freely. The natural rights movement contends that democracy violates property rights through property taxes and having the power to increase taxes and make property ownership difficult. Indeed, property reassessments—for the purposes of sustaining the expansion of government—usually threaten property rights when property owners simply cannot afford to pay the new and nearly always much higher tax assessments. The only recourse is to sell and move on.

It is hard to make any case defending government or denying that democracy is nothing but a pretext for government to diminish our liberty and personal autonomy. Governments are born out of our own fear of ourselves, such as our belief that without government our society will devolve and collapse. We will supposedly descend into chaos and debauchery. It is also hard to deny that our democracy is corrupt and corrupting. Nearly 350 years of slavery and Jim Crow make this most evident. But should liberty be our highest aspiration? Is this what the natural order of the world is revealing to us? No doubt, liberty is important. But the world's natural order also makes plain that autonomy is an illusion. The world's natural order is inherently ecological. Our well-being is bound up with the well-being of others. We are obligated to care for the well-being of others. We can accept the fact that government is corrupt and also have compassion for those who have been victimized by government under the pretext of promoting equality and diversity. Government is seductive. It releases us from the hard work of providing for ourselves and taking responsibility for our actions and lack thereof. But both rich and poor are seduced by government. To give the impression that only the poor are corrupted by government is dishonest. To also forward the view that a natural aristocracy explains the hierarchical ordering within any society is no less dishonest. There could well be a natural aristocracy among human beings, but using this device to explain success and prosperity reflects a lack of rigor. We know well that government plays an important role in allocating resources and privileges. To use autonomy to explain success also makes for poor scholarship and a morally deficient view of success. That a person becomes wealthy and successful by starting a company that burns fossil fuels and destroys the environment can never be described as successful, especially from a natural rights perspective. For what is the value of any model of success that destroys the natural world that supposedly makes for such success by giving us a natural aristocracy? In the end, liberty for the sake of only liberty makes for greed and promiscuity.

CHAPTER 25

ON THE LIMITS OF SCIENCE

STEVEN PINKER, PROFESSOR OF PSYCHOLOGY at Harvard University, believes that science is responsible for our moral evolution. It is "indispensible in all areas of human concern, including politics, the arts, and the search for meaning, purpose, and morality" (Pinker, 2013). In fact, "the worldview that guides the moral and spiritual values of an educated person today is the worldview given to us by science." Pinker claims that the "facts of science, by exposing the absence of purpose in the laws governing the universe, force us to take responsibility for the welfare of ourselves, our species, and our planet." Moreover, science makes for "a defensible morality, namely adhering to principles that maximize the flourishing of humans and other sentient beings." Pinker contends that this "humanism . . . is becoming the de facto morality of modern democracies, international organizations, and liberalizing religions, and its unfulfilled promises define the moral imperatives we face today." Further, "science has contributed—directly and enormously—to the fulfillment of these values." Indeed, "If one were to list the proudest accomplishments of our species . . . many would be gifts bestowed by science." For Pinker, science is responsible for deepening "our understanding of what it means to be human and our place in the world."

What Pinker gets correct is that science is a worldview. It reflects a certain way of perceiving and understanding the world. But what Pinker gets wrong is viewing science as only a worldview. Worldviews do much more than simply shape how we perceive and make sense of the world. Worldviews also shape how we experience the world, and all that we believe, value, and desire. Worldviews shape our sensibility, our rationality, our modality. Simply put, worldviews fashion our being, and also the thought system that comes with different kinds of being.

Pinker would have us believe that science is devoid of ideology. It is merely a worldview dedicated to the discovery of truth. But why truth rather than meaning or something else? Did the pursuit of truth come from the heavens or from human beings? Indeed, science is an ideology. It is a system of values and beliefs that human beings created. Nothing is wrong with owning this reality. Science is probably a better worldview than most. But to downplay the fact that science is still a system that human beings created is a different matter. To do so, which Pinker does, is to give the impression that science is beyond scrutiny and that the only problem with science has to do with application. In other words, the mission of science is presumably flawless. We are to assume that science represents the zenith of our potential. It is supposedly our greatest invention, and thereby responsible for our most significant achievements.

Consequently, Pinker cannot fathom why a few in academe are unwilling to embrace science. It is science, after all, that presumably saved us from "human sacrifice, witch hunts, faith healing, trial by ordeal," and other such nonrational systems. This, again, may no doubt be true. But what of the unsurpassed ecological destruction that science brought? What other worldview is responsible for as much destruction? How could science have no role in all of this destruction?

Every worldview has its own logic and coherence. Science is no different. It is incapable of doing anything that is contrary to its logic and coherence, and will tolerate no threat to either. This is how worldviews achieve stability and continuity. It is also why diversity is impossible in science. In the end, science demands that we all abide by the same rules, the same methods, the same protocols, the same standards. This is why science is incapable of asking fundamentally new questions. It can only asks questions that conform to its logic and coherence. This is why, even in the face of pending doom, worldviews are unable to change course and produce a fundamentally new knowledge. In this regard, science is no different.

Pinker would have us believe that to oppose science is to oppose enlightenment and rigorous inquiry. Presumably, only science offers a commitment to progress, regardless of whether the heavens may fall. But this is false. Also false is the idea that science is responsible for our moral evolution by saving us from nonrational movements. Eventually every ecology must either evolve or die. One way or another, change is inevitable and necessary. To credit science for our moral evolution is to miss the fact that worldviews are ecologies, and thereby bound to certain rules and rhythms. Stupidity will always come with a price.

The ecological peril of our ways makes plain that this price is now upon us. Only so much stupidity can any ecology tolerate. We now need new worldviews that are in harmony with the world's rules and rhythms. Pinker misses the fact that worldviews, in being ideological systems, are also political systems. Worldviews strive to displace other worldviews. In most cases, the process is never humane. But hegemony is the goal. We want our own worldview to dictate how the world will be perceived and understood, and how our society will be organized and resources distributed. No worldview willingly surrenders this kind of power and hegemony. Consequently, no new worldview will ever come forth without struggle and sacrifice.

Trying to dismantle and delegitimize science is futile. As with any worldview, science will recalibrate and neutralize any serious threat. Its logic and coherence will ensure that any serious threat looks strange and even insane. Indeed, these kinds of struggles between worldviews eventually move from searching for legitimacy to holding on to our sanity. We learn from history that such struggles rarely end well. We are nearly always broken, vanquished, or persecuted. Yet emergent worldviews can take heart in the fact that ecologies are hostile to hegemonies, and those that put us in conflict with the world's rules and rhythms are destined to implode.

References

Carter, S. L. (2012, September 6). It is to be hoped that proper grammar can endure. *Bloomberg Business.* http://www.bloomberg.com/news/articles/2012-09-06/it-is-to-be-hoped-that-proper-grammar-can-endure

Ferguson, N. (2011). *Civilization: The West and the rest.* New York: Penguin.

Heclo, H. (2008). *On thinking institutionally.* Boulder, CO: Paradigm.

Hoppe, H. (2001). *Democracy—The God that failed: The economics and politics of monarchy, democracy, and natural order.* New Brunswick, NJ: Transaction.

Ignatieff, M. (2001). *Human rights as politics and idolatry.* Princeton, NJ: Princeton University Press.

Kuhn, T. (1996). *The structure of scientific revolutions.* Chicago: University of Chicago Press.

Pinker, S. (2011). *The better angels of our nature: Why violence has declined.* New York: Viking.

Pinker, S. (2013). Science is not your enemy: An impassioned plea to neglected novelists, embattled professors, and tenure-less historians. *New Republic.* http://www.newrepublic.com/article/114127/science-not-enemy-humanities

About the Author

Amardo Rodriguez (Ph.D., Howard University) is a *Laura J. and L. Douglas Meredith* Professor in the Department of Communication and Rhetorical Studies at Syracuse University. His research and teaching interests explore the potentiality of emergent conceptions of communication that foreground moral, existential, and spiritual assumptions about the human condition to redefine and enlarge current understandings of democracy, diversity, and community. Publications include articles in *Journal of Intercultural Communication*, *Journal of Intergroup Relations*, *Journal of Religion and Society*, *Qualitative Report*, *Journal of Rural Community Psychology*, *Journal of Race and Policy*, *Southern Communication Journal*, and elsewhere. Books include *On Matters of Liberation (I): The Case Against Hierarchy*; *Diversity as Liberation (II): Introducing a New Understanding of Diversity*; *Communication: Colonization and the Making of a Discipline*; *On Being Human: Notes on the Human Condition*; and *Revisioning Diversity in Communication Studies*.

www.ingramcontent.com/pod-product-compliance
Lightning Source LLC
Chambersburg PA
CBHW031441160426
43195CB00010BB/813